Chaos Craft

The Wheel of the Year
in
Eight Colours

Julian Vayne
&
Steve Dee

Chaos Craft

Chaos Craft ©2014 Julian Vayne & Steve Dee

ISBN 978-0-9954904-2-0

Images (by page numbers):
31 44 72 74 76 79 82 84 87 112 115 129 131 136 143 146 154 167 169 175 177 181 192 213 217 234 242 Creative Commons/Public domain
186 ©2012 Russell Lownsbrough
204 ©2014 Greg Humphries
27 35 52 65 70 89 120 123 125 189 208 ©2012-2014 Julian Vayne
All other images, including cover, ©2012-2014 Nikki Wyrd (Pages 2 18 20 22 34 39 48 53 57 59 63 78 94 96 98 100 108 109 119 134 157 164 171 202 210 225 238 240 246)

Editing, typesetting, and design: Nikki Wyrd

First published 2015 by theblogofbaphomet.com
Second edition 2016 published by The Universe Machine, Norwich.

http://theblogofbaphomet.com/

The Universe Machine

Contents

Chaos Craft

Introduction
What (Chaos) Witches Do

This is a book of shadows. These shadows are the written marks, the trace in language of our magical explorations. These explorations of magic, of mindfulness and of mystery were undertaken within a small circle of friends calling themselves The Western Watchtower. This book represents ideas, rituals and reflections made during two years of working with a particular approach to magic, a nascent tradition perhaps, what we call the Chaos Craft (or 'The Craft of Chaos'; you pays your money...). 'Chaos', because our explorations developed within the highly innovative and syncretic approach to occultism that began in the 1970s known as 'chaos magic'. 'Craft' because we are also informed by those traditions that use this as a key term - The Craft (from the Egyptian, Hermetic, & esoteric aspects Masonry), its velvet and sometimes skyclad clad Sister tradition, Wicca, and the dark-folkish style of Traditional Witchcraft and Sabbatic Craft. At the core of this hybridisation is the simple principle of blending the neo-pagan wheel of the year (the model of the Eight Sabbats that is conventional in modern British Paganism) with the Eight Colours of Magic. The Eight Colours system is of course derived from the work of Peter J. Carroll. (See *Liber Kaos* and *The Esotericon & Portals of Chaos*.)

Our approach was also informed by the chaos magic style in terms of group structure. This method for running esoteric meetings is used in some non-aligned chaos magic groups and explicitly in the operation of the premier chaos magic Order 'The Magical Pact of the Illuminates of Thanateros' (IOT). This kind of skill-sharing model is common in the practice of the IOT, although The Western Watchtower is not exclusively an IOT Temple.

Using the combination of each colour of magic, plus the season, gave us a theme for each meeting at which all members of our group would bring a practice to share. There was no single High Priest or Priestess of our Coven. Each person contributed to the gathering. They might bring something simple to share, such as an inspirational reading suited to the season. They could bring a physical body practice, a spell casting ritual, or something much more complex. The person leading their part of the session is (in IOT-speak) 'MT' (Magister Templi)). Their job is to have created a practice that can be shared successfully (allowing for the fact that all members of the group are very experienced practitioners, often with many years involvement in occultism - thus enabling us to feel sure we're all on the same page so-to-speak). The MT is responsible for ensuring, in their part of the meeting (as far as is possible), the effectiveness, and safety of what they are presenting. While a member of the group is MT they often, to some degree, sacrifice something of their own experience in order to facilitate the space for others. Then, once they are done, another MT takes over for the next section. Sometimes people work together and the rituals or other activities are presented by multiple MTs.

Usually a number of activities would be conducted one after another. The proposed running order (of different rites and practices, typically assembled at the start of a meeting) would naturally and instinctively emerge as people described what they wanted to do. Details were recorded; name of the person acting as MT, title of the ritual, approximate duration, and any special features (e.g. whether the rite needed to be performed outside, or perhaps after nightfall, etc). Breaks from temple work would occur within the running order and, at the end of the session, time was spent relaxing and feasting. Although our group was relatively small (our largest meeting comprised 13 individuals), personnel had the option of sitting out any of the practices (as they do within the IOT methodology) if, for some reason, they felt incongruent with the aim or structure of a practice, or if they simply needed some time to reflect and rest from active ritual work.

Given the above story of the practicalities surrounding this budding Craft of Chaos, the present volume really is a proper 'Book of Shadows'. It's a mongrel esoteric text. The work of many magicians, many voices, many rituals. A mash-up, a mutant, a cyborg even; just like the Gardnerian *Book of Shadows* (a blend of Thelema, Solomonic ritual, Freemasonry, folk-tradition and more...). This book isn't about a fully card-carrying Witchcraft (although I myself am an initiated Wiccan), nor is it totally down-the-line IOT-esque chaos magic either (although a number of us are members of the IOT). But that's a good thing; hybrids give us diversity, new possibility, adaptability and, if the blend is a good one, new strengths.

Many of the essays in this book were first published at theblogofbaphomet.com which (if you're reading this in the far future) is still accessible using the distributed nanotech akashic record. Some of the material is presented here for the first time. This includes many of the key rituals about which we remained silent, while blogging with wild abandon about the rest.

Articulated at various points in this text you'll also see our emerging ideas about Left-hand Path (LHP) Occultism. This term, originally adopted by the Theosophical Society to designate baddie magicians, has been refined by insights from Tantrism, the body-centred occultism of many 20th century schools (Typhonianism and ecstatic forms of Wicca for instance), and through the work of contemporary Satanists (notably Anton LaVey, Michael Aquino and Stephen Flowers). Our reading of the LHP sees it as a term that is closely related to the Tibetan Tantric-Buddhist Vajrayāna school. Like Vajrayāna our reading of the LHP is an approach that is both personally and socially liberating. It includes the use of 'skilful means' (occult work) that uses our desires to allow us to fully understand ourselves and, paradoxically, transcend our own attempts at grasping at reality. It is a LHP that is life affirming, materialist, fluid, and situates the magician not as an isolated self (as does the LHP of Aquino and Flowers) but as a skilful, empowered, interdependent and indeed humble participant in the unfolding story of the universe coming into self-awareness.

However, these subtle philosophical points are presented - for the most part - not as a fixed set of axioms or revelatory insights, but within the workbook that is this particular Book of Shadows. They emerge as understandings garnered through reflecting on the work we did, and the innumerable conversations between times. This was a process of us watching a tradition unfold through us.

As with any magical current, the narrative of Chaos Craft is bigger than just our group (in fact during this period our Sister group in Wales also used the Chaos Craft approach in their own unique way). We have recorded what we did when we encountered this Baphometic-Luciferian-Fourth Way-Buddhist-Wiccan 'vibe' (that we call Current 729, for reasons obvious to those who are acquainted with gematria), but, what comes next; how this hybrid develops for us, and in other hands (schooled in different traditions and skilled in ways that none of the authors here are) is anyone's guess.

I sincerely hope that this book will inspire you. I have certainly been inspired by the work we've been doing and the wonderful people with whom I've shared this process. My great thanks and respect goes to Nicola Lydon and Peter Pracownik and all those beautiful people in the circle at St. Nectan's Glen in Cornwall with whom I was able to share many beautiful Pagan ceremonies during this time. My appreciation also goes out to the excellent community of pagans, medicine people, Zen-Odinists and many others who have informed, inspired and supported me in this journey.

Naturally my deepest gratitude and admiration goes out to the members of The Western Watchtower (many of whom have their rituals described in this book), and especially to Louise and TP808. I hope that I have done some measure of justice in this writing to the thoughtful, creative and powerful rites they have conceived and presented in our Coven.

Finally my grateful thanks and love to Steve Dee, one of the most outstanding magicians I've ever met and a person I am blessed to have as a friend.

JV

Thoughts on Chaos Craft...

When I read back through these entries and the themes that connect them, I was struck by the degree to which they address a diversity of concepts, while at the same time containing a number of repeating motifs. For me it would run contra to the reality of our process as a group of practitioners to try and homogenize our methods into some coherent whole and deny its inherent complexity. When we look at traditions like the Hermetic Order of the Golden Dawn or Gardnerian Wicca, while there may be defining pieces of liturgy or stylistic approach that define their parameters, we cannot escape the plurality of sources and techniques that they employ.

Processes that make heady use of synthesis and syncretism are rarely problematic for the Chaos magician. When diverse cultures and ideologies co-exist, the dynamics of how they shift and influence each other often provide the magician or mimetic engineer with a new energy wave on which to surf. What I think this volume tries to clarify is the way in which we can employ this insight more consciously, so as to explore interconnection and the benefits of creative hybridisation.

It may be that the discomfort with syncretism that some experience is more about the pace at which it occurs rather than it happening at all. In contrast to a more organic process whereby two or more differing perspectives interact over time, perhaps our sense of psychic indigestion relates to the rate in which we are bombarded by a plethora of competing worldviews day in, day out.

In trying to tease apart the possible differences between the process of syncretism and that of hybridisation, one of the primary differences seems to be the degree of consciousness brought to the activity. While syncretism often occurs unconsciously via proximity, hybridisation usually involves the deliberate splicing together of at least two differing perspectives in order to produce a new entity that functions more effectively than the original systems within the context of which it is developed. In reflecting on the development of the Chaos Craft approach I have begun my own process of trying to identify some of the common traits that might be shared by those engaging in conscious hybridisation. Some of my suggestions are as follows:

1.   A sense of vision related to the hybrid being proposed - rather than it being just an amusing 'mash-up', the individual or group involved feel that something important is being offered and that there is a sense of aesthetic coherence between the paths involved; e.g. for me the combining of a chaotic approach with a more Wiccan style of practice related to my desire to balance innovation with a more earth-focused spirituality.

2.   A desire to engage as thoroughly as possible with the primary source material of whichever traditions or ideologies that are being combined.

3.   A high degree of transparency with regards to both the sources being worked with and the process of combination itself.

Probably like any good art, the sacred technician seeking to work with these hybridising processes needs to combine both vision and discipline. Vision ensures that the endeavour itself is fuelled by the uprising of creative energy inspired by the need to contextualize spiritual ideals. Discipline hopefully reduces the likelihood of simply using religious buzzwords in order to legitimise personal whim.

In the light of our desire to engage in this style of working, it got me to thinking back over the discussions that we had with each other and with other magicians within our group, with regards to the main drivers or goals that led to the emergence of this style of working. While these are of course subject to change and evolution, my own hypothesis as to why we pursued this Chaos-Craft fusion were as follows:

♦ Seeking to work expressly with the alchemical/Gnostic mysteries that we see as being connected to the glyph and myth of Baphomet. Baphomet presents us with a mystery - an unfinished God whose backstory seems to be made up of overheard whispers and half-truths. Hir mysteries seem to hold within themselves the conjoining of male, female, bestial and human. The dissolving and reforming that seems innate to the mysteries of Solve et Coagula acknowledge the permeable boundaries of the body and the fluidity of queered discourses.

♦ Experiencing these mysteries as having an initiatory telos with regards our own personal development and unfolding.

♦ That while this working is more LHP in aesthetic, it is within the tantric understanding of this concept, i.e. our awakening to the mysteries of self and the divine are largely within the biosphere and emergent as a result of an evolution within it. These insights potentially represent our own iteration of a type of hermetic/integral panpsychism.

♦ That we choose to view it as a Witches' craft in that it is magical, ecstatic and holistic rather than just being concerned with magical technology. As we meet so we weave - not only do we construct magical tools, destroy sigils and create initiatory artefacts, we also knit new meaning and forge systemic links that acknowledge the phenomenon of group practice as well as honouring the unique contribution of each individual.

♦ That the iterative process of the wheel of the year and the colours of magick represent the mysteries of both life and death, and that in attuning to this cycle we gain profound insights into the nature of impermanence and the oscillating nature of the great work. Meaning can be located at once within the imminent reality of the biosphere, while at the same time realising that space-ship Earth sits within a Kosmic context that has signalled aspiration for millennia. We are both "right here right now" and also "here to go". To sit with such paradoxes produces a resonance/dissonance that fuels our further exploration.

While the technology of our magical praxis is still carried out with the type of rigour that one has come to associate with the CM approach (the scientific method and results magic), the Chaos Craft approach also acknowledges the importance of celebration and devotion as being key components in understanding how 'deep magick' works. This is a process of personal and collective enrichment as much as it is a sorcerous surging outward.

The insights and revelations gained have been as part of an emergent group process. As much as we, as individuals, have gained and expressed wisdom as a result of the work undertaken, it is in the heady process of these ideas being shared that greater depth is accessed. When we as a coven have met during the turning of the year, the dynamic interplay between its members has allowed the development of a group mind that has often allowed us to access new vistas of collective gnosis.

While as a magician I take responsibility for the work that I bring to share in a group setting, it has invariably been enriched by the interplay between those colleagues I have been so privileged to work with ☺ Personally I would never underestimate the profound magical potency of deep friendship, irreverent laughter and a large teapot! My thanks go to the wonderful Mr Vayne and my other beloved co-conspirators.

SD

"Let My People Go!"
Witchcraft as a Liberation Theology?

Most religious systems are ultimately designed as systems of liberation. They may differ in terms of what they think we are in need of liberation from (Sin, Desire, Ignorance, Maya etc.), but my own reading is that they are seeking to offer some sort of solution to our haunting sense of discomfort. While such answers may begin with the insights of an enlightened individual, they rarely remain as such. Given time to evolve and gaze outwards many religious traditions develop a Mahayanist dimension where the liberation of the individual demands a response to the "other". Bodhisattva vows and states of kenosis (self-emptying) are no guarantee of socio-political engagement beyond well-intended paternalism, but they can often provide the basis for developing more empowered notions of interdependence and systemic awareness.

The 1950s and 60s witnessed an important movement within the Roman Catholic Church in South America, when people who were engaged with the coal face of day-to-day hardship re-envisioned the gospel message, in relation to political and economic oppression. The Liberation of the Israelites from Egypt and the Gospel message of Christ were viewed as narratives of freedom whereby "the downtrodden were lifted up" (*Luke 1:52*). With the birth of Liberation Theology in the works of Boff, Gutierrez et al, past dogmas were no longer sufficient, and the rigours of true discipleship were now to be measured in terms of deeds or praxis. As Desmond Tutu powerfully observed; "If you are neutral in situations of injustice, then you have chosen the side of the oppressor."

In recent discussions with some of my siblings from our coven, I've been wondering again about the relationship between liberation and this thing we call 'Witchcraft'. What does Witchcraft claim to offer liberation from? And is it able to embrace or embody liberation at a collective level?

Much ink has been spilt in attempting to define what Witchcraft may or may not have been, and while we may have re-appropriated it from accusing lips, its evocative potency often evades concrete categorisation.

Cognitive Liberty:

In his *Europe's Inner Demons*, Norman Cohn masterfully analyses the evidence with regards the likelihood of the Witches' Sabbath having any basis in historic fact. Cohn concludes that it was highly unlikely that the fevered imaginings of persecuting clerics had any foundation in relation to some sort of denominational adherence to a set of pan-European 'night ecstasies'. What seems more evident is that their actions were overwhelmingly directed at other groups of people who considered themselves Christians. While It is almost inevitable that some of these Christians practised magic (and by doing so, demonstrated their humanity), the fear projected by these clerics was more often motivated by an ungodly desire to control.

The Church's ability to control would always be challenged by the heterodoxy of groups such as the Cathars, the Albegensians and the Beguines, the power of their subjective gnostic experiences being valued above any external authority. Whatever the degree of adherence to such beliefs by the mainstream of society, the ideas that such outsider groups represented, embodied a type of cognitive liberty that eroded the hold of any centralised hegemony.

While we may not buy into Michelet's idealisation of the Witch as Satanic freedom fighter, there is something subversive contained within even the simplest act of folk magic. To express a sense of agency through a magical act that uses means outside or beyond the Church's recognised sacraments is to commit an act of heteropraxy.

Within the collective psyche of Europe, the Witch has often acted as an icon of disturbance and freedom. The projected fantasies of clerics and folkloric imaginings often allude to something dark, disturbing and subversive. The Witch often acts as an attractor for the shadow aspects of those cultures within which they are suspected of dwelling. They seem to be scapegoats onto whose heads the repressed longings of society are spoken. In bearing the weight of such dangerous passions they often hold a position on the outer edge of social and ethical evolution.

Not a scapegoat

In seeking to own their own sense of spiritual and moral agency, magicians have often played a catalysing role in pushing the boundaries of moral acceptability. When we consider a figure like Crowley and his catalysing impact on 20th century culture, while his personal chaos may still make him less than attractive as a role model, the bisexuality and entheogenic exploration that then caused such outrage are now far less contentious.

To question orthodoxies and seek new means for personal exploration will inevitably threaten those for whom stability is paramount. Those of us who consciously embrace identities such as 'Witch', 'Magician' or 'Gnostic' are honour bound to aid our cultures' development, in prodding them to embrace diversity, multiplicity and liberty. When we take on this mantle we must remain awake to the reality that we both represent the freedom that so many seek, and, that we still risk being scapegoated by those who would seek to control.

SD

Chaos Magic and The Pagan Year

There are eight Sabbats and eight colours of magic (in the system devised by Pete Carroll) and so (as someone steeped in both the Wiccan Paganism and chaotic/eclectic occultism) it makes sense to me to explore how these systems can relate to each other. Of course the esoteric cake can be cut any number of ways and so this is simply my (current) serving suggestion. A Brother of mine in Germany has been working on similar lines and has come up with some slightly different ideas, and that's all good. There is an immediate difference between these models in that the eight rays of the chaosphere are simply indicative of the many, many arrows which rush out from the singularity of Kia.

But if we stick to the 8-fold symbolism for now...

We start with the 'conventional' colours of magick as given by Pete in *Liber Kaos*:

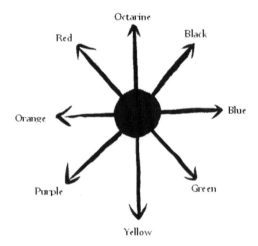

The Eight Colours of Magic

I asked Pete recently why he chose the locations for the colours as given in his diagram above. Of course these energies/colours/styles are in opposing (or perhaps 'complementary' pairs). However the diagram doesn't fit with either the Qabalistic system (if you overlay the chaosphere on Isaac Luria's ten-balls-and-twenty-two-sticks model of the Tree it doesn't match up); neither is there any obvious astrological relationship (like the order of the planets as given on the heptagram shown in Crowley's *Book of Thoth*). Mr Carroll told me that the order was 'essentially arbitrary' and therefore by changing the position of the colours (while maintaining the complementary pairs) I wouldn't be 'committing any great heresy' (phew!).

So my proposal is that the order of colours as given by Pete Carroll can be re-arranged to give a neat fit between the core symbolism of each Pagan Sabbat and each colour of magick. I've only been using this model for a few months, but by working with love (the type of love that allows a mother to nourish her baby with milk) at Imbolc, and the more cerebral vibe of opening out my ability to communicate at the most recent equinox, it seems to be working out for me.

This type of re-configuration is, of course, one of the delights of modern magickal culture. We can create blends that suit our own spiritual tastes. Rather than going from system to system, abandoning one psychic structure to invest in a nice new shiny one, we can also manufacture hybrids. The alchemy of birthing such ceremonial chimera helps to keep our styles of magick strong and vigorous. And as a dedicated chaos magician and witch I'd rather be a robust mongrel than a sickly pedigree!

JV

The symbolic links between the directions and colours are:

<u>Yule</u> - Octarine, the Sun at Midnight, the paradox and play of festival, the birth of the God Son. North.

<u>Imbolc</u> - Green, love and sacrifice, parenthood, the promise of Spring. Northeast.

<u>Spring Equinox</u> - Orange, the incoming power of the year, East.

<u>Beltane</u> - Purple, sex. Southeast.

<u>Midsummer</u> - Yellow, the self, the waking consciousness. South.

<u>Lammas</u> - Red, agriculture, war, John Barleycorn must die. Southwest.

<u>Autumn Equinox</u> - Blue, wealth, reflecting on what we have gathered in the year. West.

<u>Samhain</u> - Black, death. Northwest.

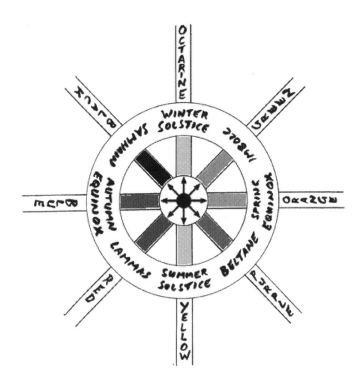

The Wheel of Chaos

When Chaos Magick Gets Deep....

I've been pondering of late the tendency for Chaos/Post-modern magickal practitioners to seek more meaningful depth within a specific spiritual paradigm. Folks who have previously focused their efforts on surfing the rapids of our ever shifting culture seem to be increasingly looking back to more ancient paths as a way of enriching their journeys.

Chaos Magic (CM) has been the form of Magic that in my view best embodies the Postmodern zeitgeist. Via its use of contemporary culture and the scientific method, it has managed to boot out much of the stuffy pseudo-masonic baggage that pervaded much of the magical scene. In reflecting the postmodern emphasis on relativity and adaptation many Magicians in the 80s and 90s felt freed by the realisation that belief itself was a magickal weapon. These budding psychonauts could add belief shifting to their personal arsenal without feeling that they had to abandon reason.

Yet increasingly it seems that this isn't enough for many of us. Moving now to the second decade of the 21st century we see an ever increasing interest in 'traditional' witchcraft, dusty tomes on Solomonic magic and various brands of radical traditionalism. With such a preoccupation concerning times and things past, one has to wonder whether Chaos Magick (like Punk Rock) is dead.

When I've sat down and talked to friends who've been involved in CM for any length of time (5 years+) I've noticed that many of us (if not most of us) have chosen to deepen our spiritual journeys by pursuing initiatory work within a specific historic tradition. Whether Heathenry, Tantra, Voudou or Wicca, people are obviously wanting more than Chaos Magick alone is (apparently) offering. Why?

At its worst the Chaos approach can reflect not only the flexibility of the postmodern but also its superficiality and implicit consumerism. As we push our trolley around the spiritual supermarket seeking to fill our Kia-shaped hole, do we stock up on the nutritious sustenance offered by deep reflection on the Upanishads, or do we neck a pile of spiritual sugar highs that ultimately give us a gnostic hangover? People who were attracted to CM because it actually did something and sought to measure its effectiveness (results magick anyone?) began to long for something more. In the midst of all this paradigm shifting busyness, is there a place for 'being' and soul development as well as doing and incessantly changing?

So why stay involved with Chaos Magick? After at least 12 years, bottom line, for me it's the holism. CM for me manages to engage with culture in a manner that embodies Crowley's project of scientific illuminism - "the method of science, the aim of religion". When so many esoteric traditions seem bogged down in colloquialisms and the tenets of faith, CM seeks to strip things back so as to help identify the technologies used by traditions and the commonalities that exist between them. Like the Perennial philosophy and its contemporary Integral manifestations, CM seeks to hold a 'Meta' position that steps back and notices. All our beliefs and practices are ultimately tools for awakening: "a finger pointing at the moon". For me the Chaos approach helps me hold a bigger vision, and enables me to hold my obsessions more loosely.

The depth and romanticism that tradition provides may well be essential in avoiding some trendy but ultimately futile spiritual dead-end street. But if CM can become a tool that we use skilfully, it may be a key to developing inner poise. This poise allows us to be responsive to the changing world around us and to escape the pitfalls of faith commitments based on past certainties that can no longer be relied on.

SD

Slow Chaos...

A friend recently claimed surprise when during an exchange concerning magickal experimentation, I cried off a certain technique due to its lack of basis in 'tradition'. "You're a Chaos Magician, you're supposed to be endlessly syncretistic and innovative!" Well, yes and no.

As I said in the previous section "When Chaos Magick gets deep..." and its questioning of whether buying into the postmodern spirit uncritically is sustainable for those of us seeking to develop spiritual depth (or Soul as Hillman would put it): The type of hyper-accelerated paradigm shifting that many associate with CM may have a role in loosening our reliance on outdated certainties and dogma, but I wonder if it's time to slow down.

The realisation that certain aspects of Western culture may be moving too quickly for their own good is not a new one. In response to fast food, quickie sex, the never-ending pursuit of a faster internet connection, the Slow movement was born. Rather than increased mindfulness being limited to a set of internal practices, the Slow movement challenges us to wonder what would happen if such a mindful perspective was brought to bear on the whole of our lives. What would our eating habits look like, our transport arrangements, our approach to child-care?

Now there is always the danger that new insights become dogma, but the general principles of greater awareness to regional context, levels of consumption and quality over quantity are certainly a necessary challenge to my lifestyle. Do I seek endless piles of 'stuff' to fill the sense of internal ache, or can I pause and truly take stock of what's going on around me? As someone with a fairly intense work ethic, how do I step back and become less hyperactive and more intentional?

When I seek to apply a Slow perspective to the types of activity associated with Chaos Magick where does it get me? Because of CM's connection to the postmodern zeitgeist, it can be easy to assume that the approach is unavoidably accelerated via its quick and dirty punk rock approach! CM will always be pragmatic in its sorcerous focus on getting things done, but as someone who still really likes the approach, I believe that it can grow up and move beyond scatter-gun spiritual consumerism.

The genius of Chaos Magick for me lies in its understanding of belief as a tool and in its emphasis on the contemporary. CM, like all magickal systems, relies on romanticism to a certain degree, but it doesn't long for some past golden age - it demands that we Work with what's in front of us. In placing its emphasis on the present however, it also faces the danger of mirroring societies' excesses and losing touch with its context. Personally I need more, and as I grow older and my magick works its wyrd, so my engagement with this tradition needs to evolve. Therefore my Chaos Magick needs to slow down.

Marti the Mindful Mollusc - totem of Slow Chaos

What this means for each of us seeking new depth will of course be unique. Like my use of fossil fuels or hours spent 'working for the Man' few of us appreciate having our choices prescribed. What's probably most helpful at this point is to outline some of the ways that this Slow Chaos might be shaping up my own spiritual/magickal practice:

Working with each paradigm to a greater depth:

CM as an approach is renowned for its technique of shifting belief systems and world views. Its desire to stand back and comprehend the technology and mechanisms of magick outside of a faith position often allows it to see the parallels and potential connections between differing paradigms. Critics of this approach may rightly wonder whether jumping between paradigms actually allows the magician to experience the challenges and depths that prolonged work with one system can produce.

As someone who is fairly syncretistic by nature I am usually quick to cross-fertilize systems and seek creative means for cross-breeding to strengthen my already mongrel magick. Whilst recognising this I also realise that I have to slow down and let a tradition speak to me on its own terms. I need to internalise the hard lessons so that I am not simply flitting between systems, creating the illusion of progress in the midst of my frenzied busyness.

Seeking both Acceptance and Change:

In many forms of psychotherapy (my day job) one of the primary dialectics that needs to be held in tension, is that which exists between acceptance and change. If all therapy does is accept, it will never be truly healing, and if all it does is ask for change without truly listening to reality as it is for the client, then it is both an imposition and a misuse of power. How, in my spiritual life, can I access this place of acceptance rather than bleeding myself psychically dry through endless sorcerous 'doing'?

In the magickal group in which 1 work, this need to seek means for cultivating greater acceptance has led to an on-going engagement with mindfulness practice and states of receptive magick. Whether working with acceptance of the Self, or a situation we hope eventually to change, taking our time to listen more closely is likely to make our gnosis all the more potent.

Sensitivity to Context and the Movement of Time:

Julian in his "Chaos Magick and the Pagan Year" (above) has already started mapping how the multi-faceted glyph of the Chaos star might relate to the 8 fire festivals and the natural movements of life perceived in time and space. The Slow movement asks us to consider the idea of place, and how our bodies and lives are interwoven with our context and natural environment.

Personally 1 find myself interested in how we can harmonize this adventurous, experimental form of magick with sensitivity to the land and the phase of the year we are working within. Rather than the shape of our collective sorcery or ritual being determined by whim or fortune, could our work flow into the channel of yellow mid-summer ego-magick or the lusty purple hues of Beltane?

The importance of the armchair:

Philip Carr-Gomm in his excellent *The English Book of Magic* speaks of the importance of the armchair in the development of the magician. While people may dismiss those who spend time reflecting, reading, thinking and musing, Philip in his wisdom sees such critics as embodying "an undignified utilitarianism." We need time to dream, to let our ideas percolate, to let parts of our psyche lie fallow for a season.

Phil Hine has noted the creeping work ethic that seems to be part of Western occultism - more to learn, more to do, more, more, more. Most magickal orders stress that they are only interested in "highly motivated individuals", and while not dismissing this, sometimes we need to praise Bob and embrace the Slack! My guess is that most of us got involved in Magick because we dreamt and wondered; perhaps we need to dream once more - get thee to an armchair!

So there you have it, some wonderings about Slow and how it might shape and challenge our postmodern forms of Magickal practice. One of the great things for me about Current 23 is the way it seeks to allow diversity and freedom - I offer these musings in the same spirit - not a new set of prescriptions, rather some sketches that I hope will invite friendly conversation and wondering.

SD

In the Mood for Witchcraft

The other day I was hanging out in the lovely 'Labyrinth Books' in Glastonbury, eavesdropping on a conversation between two dedicated Kenneth Grant fans. They were waxing lyrical about how they really loved his later books because they were "so weird" that they seemed to alter the consciousness of the reader. As these two Typhonian chums chatted, one of them confessed that he was pretty much done with group work and Orders but still found great value in the mood that Grant's work evoked for him.

While my own approach to magic is decidedly experiential, and I'm interested in ritual drama, I found myself empathising with the lovers' of spooky books. When we encounter a work that allows us access to alien insight, the sense of taboo and dis-ease that they engender can be a decidedly magical experience. I've found myself growing increasingly interested in the importance of magical mood: how we cultivate it within ritual space, and also how this mysterious sense of 'feel' can often pervade our attempts to capture concepts and identities as enigmatic as contemporary Witchcraft.

Some moody witches.

Magical systems such as Wicca and the Golden Dawn make considerable use of both the sensual and the poetic in order to charge ritual atmosphere. Whether it be the evocative folk lore of the English countryside or the elaborate Qabalistic correspondences of 777, both of these systems invest real effort in ensuring that the ritual arc builds in a way that is congruent with the ultimate goal in mind. At best, such efforts seem less about following a script and more about cultivating an atmosphere that directs intent and allows connection to potent, often unconscious drivers.

In its mission to strip back the "what works" components of magical practice, Chaos Magick has got top marks for identifying and describing the techniques of modern shamanic practice. Arguably, what it has not been so strong on, is understanding the importance that Romantic sensibility plays in allowing soul to permeate these practices. At times, the Chaos Magickal preoccupation with the scientific method has left it vulnerable to a type of reductionism that is somewhat ironic given its connection to postmodernism. Following Heidegger, Postmodernism's radical subjectivity is posited on sensitivity to mood. Rather than over-relying on the meta-narratives of Modernity, sensitivity to mood is critical due to its importance in helping us determine how we find ourselves in our world.

In thinking specifically how this idea of mood might relate to deepening my own connection to the Witchcraft current I've got to wondering whether there is a shared sense of atmospheric sensibility that connects those that use the "W" word. While many people expend huge amounts of energy in border disputes between various forms of magical activity that share the moniker "Witchcraft", I wonder if evocative descriptors such as earthy, receptive, lunar and erotic might provide more valuable connective tissue than the claims and counter-claims regarding lineage.

When I think about my own sense of what means for me to connect to the Witch current I'm amazed by the complex collage of images and ideas that contribute toward this need - grainy 1970s *News of the World* nudity, Alexandrian Wicca,

Michelet's Satanic Witch, Starhawk's *Spiral Dance*, *The Cauldron* magazine, Chumbley Lithographs; the list goes on. For me the path of the Witch speaks of the sabbatic dreamscape, the dark feminine, and the fecund earth. Of course I want to access the best that primary source material and scholarship have to offer, but neither do I want to lose the inexact 'sense' of potency that keeps drawing me back to the Witches' craft.

Heidegger recognised that our process of understanding is a circular, repetitive but progressive act of interpretation. Our 'being' in the world is not a sterile state in our heads; rather it is a process of interaction with other people and things. Our connection to the world is not as a result of thought alone; rather it also involves an attunement to mood at both an individual and collective level. This circular process fits well with understanding Witchcraft - new information and insights are folded back in on themselves and the wheel of the year provides a macrocosmic opportunity for deepening our understanding through repetition.

The journey through the maze of pre-Christian pagan practices, the fevered imaginings of inquisitors and Neo-pagan revivalism feels entirely in keeping with my ongoing process of understanding. This desire to remain sensitive to the mood of Witchcraft is a spiral journey into deep time, it twists and turns, and my eyes need time to adjust to differing levels of light.

This feels far less about pinning Witchcraft to a board in a sterile eureka moment, more a mad pursuit across the landscape as it comes in and out of view.

SD

Some landscape, yesterday

On Seeing Witches in a Black Mirror...

I recently bought a black mirror from the extraordinary witch, writer and academic Levannah Morgan. Levannah, as visitors to many Pagan events in Britain will know, is also the creator of a wonderful array of homemade, beautifully crafted objects. These range from what are clearly ritual tools (like my mirror), through to charms, knitted hats and socks which, though ostensibly simple clothing, are undoubtedly magickal objects in their own right. In this sense Levannah straddles the worlds of the Wicca (she's a High Priestess of many years standing) and what some call 'Traditional Witchcraft' (which we might briefly define as being the use of folk magic).

The witch's mirror

The relationship between 'The Craft' (i.e. Wicca) and 'The Craft' (i.e. Traditional Witchcraft), is one where I've observed a fair amount of contention. For instance, one of the

Traditional Witchcraft facebook groups I belong to (arguably the most venerable group in that social media forum) sets out its stall by stating (in one of those pinned post thingies) that it is emphatically not a group for people interested in Wicca. The whole vibe of Traditional Craft (aside of discussions about which is the most ancient of its facebook manifestations) is one of toads, skulls, horned spirits, circumambulations, spelling coven 'cuveen' etc, etc. Now I'm down with all that; I love a bit of folksy style magick the same as the next wizard who happens to live in an 18th century West Country cottage. However when I actually look at this style in relation to the work of the Wiccans I know (of whom Levannah is one) I find it hard to see more than the narcissism of minor differences between the assumed distinctions of Traditional Craft versus Wicca. Read, for instance the engaging book *Traditional Witchcraft* by Gemma Gary. A likeable vision of the Craft which feels like a more folksy (and of course West Country orientated) version of the classic *Mastering Witchcraft* by Paul Huson. However if one were to compare say, *Eight Sabbats for Witches* by Janet and Stewart Farrar with Gemma's *Traditional Witchcraft* - certainly there are differences, but these are greatly outweighed by the similarities.

Now one of the criticisms of Wicca by Traditional Craft people, is that Wicca can be 'fluffy'; of course by that they mean that it can emerge as a 'love and light' focused gentle spiritual tradition which doesn't have the earthy scent that Traditional Crafters imagine suffuses their preferred style. Various allegations are made against this 'fluffy craft'; that it's not much more than a superficial, product orientated life-style choice. You can get your Wicca off the shelf, mediated through the work of writers such as Silver Ravenwolf et al. Thing is that for every example of vapid consumerism by 'Wiccans' I can find just as many examples of similar behaviour within Traditional Craft culture.

So it seems obvious to me that a superficial engagement with any spiritual tradition says more about the person doing the engaging, and not necessarily much about the tradition in itself.

Another aspect of the Wicca/Traditional Craft dichotomy arises from that fascinating word 'religion'. Wicca is, in some sense, a religion (though my preferred understanding would characterise it as a 'mystery religion', closer to the classical sense of 'mystery' described recently by Ronald Hutton in a lecture at the Pagan Federation Devon and Cornwall conference). Traditional Crafters, while generally being of an animist bent are, it seems, typically more concerned with operative magick (often of the type described by chaos magicians as 'sorcery'). They frequently acknowledge (unless they have some really out-there fantasies about secret Sabbats being celebrated on hilltops in the Middle Ages) that the operative witchcraft of the past (or folk magic, to use what I feel is a more accurate term) was done by people who would probably have identified themselves as Christians.

Meanwhile Wicca, particularly in parts of the United States, has made the fully-fledged transition into a church or denomination of Paganism. This is perhaps (and I'd love to hear the thoughts of North American witches about this) because religion plays a different role in American society than it does in British culture. The question 'which church do you go to?' is an important component in getting to know someone in the USA, whereas in Britain it's unlikely to be an item for discussion at all. American religion plays a critical role in social identity and so the creation of a neo-Pagan Wiccan 'church' (with all that means) makes total sense. However to the British Traditional Crafter this all looks very suspicious, and a long way away from solitary rituals involving rhyming charms and black cat bones.

But in the reflection of the black mirror such divisions begin to blur. Here I am, an initiated Gardnerian/Alexandrian Wiccan and chaos magician making use of a tool fashioned by the skilled hand of my Sister. Is this Traditional Craft, Chaos Magick or Wicca in action - could it perhaps be all three?

JV

Future Mythology

The late, great pagan author Isaac Bonewitz once mused that he thought that Druids would be the chaplains on the U.S. Enterprise. This always appealed to my inner geek as I visualised a heady mash-up of ancient priests and warp-drive technology; the myths of the ancestors forced to throw new shapes as their archetypal force meets new realities.

As Pagans, Gnostics and other magical types we have some interesting conundrums to engage with as we seek to locate sources of authority and inspiration. On one hand many of us struggle with mythic sources being given some sort of scriptural authority (the *Edda*, *Parzival*, the first *Star Wars* trilogy), and yet many of us want to anchor our spirituality in something more substantial than new age whim or consumerism.

We ain't going to Goa...

The Romanticism that seems to be key to our current perception of the past arguably runs throughout the majority of contemporary religious traditions. Everything from "the early church did it like this...." to the imagined sabbatic activities of the Witch cult rely to some extent on the projections and agendas of those engaging with the material. Personally I don't feel that this is a bad thing, merely something that needs to be acknowledged. As a good Jungian and Process theologian I thrive on the idea that religious expression is an emergent manifestation of humanity's engagement with nature and consciousness - such engagement will inevitably contain our fears and foibles as well as our highest aspirations.

Most mythologies hold within them the unfolding dance of a culture's evolution; chaos versus order, transcendent versus imminent, the corporate need versus the individual's awakening. As we look back to the ancestors in order to understand how we have arrived at where we are now, we need to realise that this is a process in which the dynamics of conflict and resolution continue still. Some may wish to idealise the past as some static wholegrain utopia, but the types of conflict present within much mythology represent the dialectical process of evolution where new realities are forged and then in turn challenged themselves.

Myth is important because its reinterpretation represents a subtle re-imagining of how we in the present engage with shared dilemmas that are endlessly repeated. In blending the historian's observation with the artist's flare, myth provides us with a less linear gateway for discovering truth, what Joseph Campbell called "metaphors of spiritual potentiality". In contrast to dogma or isolated philosophical ascent, the dream-like impressionism that myth often evokes allows us to access something deep and mysterious within ourselves. The fuzzy edges of mythic thinking allow us to burst the bubble of perfectionism and rigid certainty as we revel in their multiple perspectives and imprecision.

Whatever aeonic schema or eschatological endgame we choose to buy into, the unfolding evolution of a mythic narrative often reflects the subtle shifts and changing needs of a culture. Whether we are sitting ringside watching Set and Osiris slug it out or viewing the smoke rise from an ever repeating Ragnarok, the interface between these deep myths and our daily experience inevitably forces our gods to remanifest.

It is of course critical that we engage thoroughly with the best source material available so that the heartwood of our spirituality allows us to be both strong and flexible, but equally we must be wary of concretizing our perception of lore in some sort of pagan fundamentalism. The sustainability of these subtle mutations will probably be best served by adopting a Slow model of development. We will need to be awake to our contexts and also the sense of 'fit' as we explore new ways of working with mythic realities. We will need a relationship with the spirits of this material so as to ensure a true depth of evolution rather than a short-sighted wish fulfilment.

In pondering the future of myth and how our deep stories will change in the future, it is my view that we as Gnostics and magicians will be at the experimental front edge of this process. Those myths with a fuller history may rightly be slower to evolve; the degree of consciousness directed toward them giving them a greater archetypal density. Other stories however may be more flexible!

In *The Book of Baphomet*, Nikki and Julian put forward the idea that part of Baphomet's suitability as a god of our age is primarily due to hir being a glyph or image in search of a mythology. This is part of hir appeal as a deity for those of us who choose to work with hir - we sort through the scattered fragments of backstory trying to make sense of our experience viewed through the lenses of Levi's infamous depiction and our own ritual experimentation. This sense of mythic fluidity and shape-shifting is arguably why ze proves to be such a vital patron for those of us undertaking magickal exploration. The chaotes are not alone in this endeavour, other brave imaginings are also at work within occulture; be it the re-birth of Lucifer via the twisting paths of traditional witchcrafts, or the re-visioned role of Beelzebub as awakened cosmonaut seeking out bold, new transmissions. While such experiments may be at risk of faddishness, these more recent embodiments of the collective unconscious are often strange attractors for the aspirations of culture.

For the druid on the Enterprise, Cernunnos may be the Lord of the inter-dimensional space travel and their Ogham may also include extra-terrestrial flora. Our gods are alive and in living they change - how could it be otherwise?!

SD

Strange Revelations

I was recently sitting around a table drinking tea with some fellow magicians (a favourite pastime of mine!) discussing those films and works of fiction that have wriggled their way into our personal magical systems. I guess Chaos magicians are renowned for this sort of approach - taking inspiration from contemporary cultural references and valuing them as valid channels for pursuing personal and collective gnosis. In a fantastic version of geek cage fighting, we traded off verbatim quotations from David Lynch's *Dune* script and wondered how we could use sleeping bags to act as the giant sand worms of Arakis.

Recent mention has been made at this blog about folks working with the Cthulhu mythos and the way in which Lovercraft's imagery allows a vivid exploration of the existential angst and alienation that many of us experience. Having done a bit of work with the Mythos I must confess that it's really not my thing. As much as I like HPL's writing and the bizarre cosmology he envisaged, I don't find myself rushing to spend time hanging out in his universe. Perhaps because I spend most of my working life wrestling with psychic pain and descents into 'madness', I prefer to spend my leisure time avoiding cosmic terror! It may just be that my middle-class aesthetics lean more to facing the universe on a Zen cushion rather than having my soul sucked out by the tentacled one.

This idea that our spirituality is innately shaped by contemporary cultural references is hardly surprising. When I think about my own timeline, it's hard to get past the tsunami-sized impact of both punk rock and *Star Wars*. 1977 you rock! Joseph Campbell via George Lucas has allowed the hero's journey to become one of the primary metaphors for 21st century psychological development. The battling dualism of the Force seems to make more sense of our attempts at psychological integration than idealised monotheisms. Some of us may harbour more Sith-like passions than the straight-laced Jedi (bunch of goody-goodies!), but most of us are still seeking to bring balance to the Force.

Revelation rarely sits still. I've recently been having a fairly thorough pummelling via the work of Octavia Butler. For those not in the know, Butler was an awesome sci-fi writer who, as a black woman, brought a vital voice to the genre. Through her work she sought to address themes around race, gender and community. Whether via polyamorous alien/human interbreeding (*Lilith's Brood*) or a necessary shot in the arm for the vampire novel (*The Fledgling*), she brought new perspectives and raised crucial questions in the minds of her readers.

The series that's currently blowing me away is the *Earthseed* duology. In these books Octavia depicts a young woman's battle to find meaning in a dystopian landscape in which the outdated faith of her parents has ceased to make sense. *The Parable of the Sower* and *The Parable of the Talents* describes her experience of receiving the revelation of *Earthseed*, a new theology that sees God as a chaotic process of change that the awakened can shape via their intent. Each chapter of the books begin with quotations from *Earthseed*, and what follows are a couple of quotations to give you a flavour:

Consider: Whether you're a human being, an insect, a microbe, or a stone, this verse is true.

All that you touch
You Change.

All that you Change
Changes you.

The only lasting truth
Is Change.

God
Is Change.

(Octavia E. Butler, *Parable of the Sower*)

God is Power
Infinite,
Irresistible,
Inexorable,
Indifferent.

And yet, God is pliable-
Trickster,
Teacher,
Chaos,
Clay.

God exists to be shaped.

God is Change.

(Octavia E. Butler, *Parable of the Sower*)

The divine word or Logos need not be limited to sacred texts - whether they be the *Bhagavad Gita*, *Liber AL* or *Principia Discordia*. We will probably all have books, music, films and people within which we find a rich source of inspiration, but the Mystery may even burst through during *The X-Factor* or a Murdoch tabloid. Nothing is inerrant and Everything is useable!

The incoming of gnosis can come in many forms - whether via conscious spiritual endeavour or the overheard snatches of a stranger's conversation, when the lights come on and revelation ignites in our skulls we find ourselves back at that crossroads of the present moment. For that conversation with our muse to flow we need to find a way forward. We don't always get it right, but the internal pull of Will drags us onwards. May we all be brave enough to keep listening.

I must not fear. Fear is the mind-killer. Fear is the little-death that brings total obliteration. I will face my fear. I will permit it to pass over me and through me. And when it has gone past I will turn the inner eye to see its path. Where the fear has gone there will be nothing. Only I will remain.

Bene Gesserit Litany Against Fear.

SD

Colours of Chaos

Blue
The Blue Equinox

As explained previously Chaos Craft involves using the Pagan Wheel of the Year and the eight colours of magick as the container within which a bring-and-share model of running a magickal meeting is deployed. Using this approach individuals get the opportunity to bring their own practice or ritual work to explore with others. They lead that section of the meeting, acting as Master/Mistress of the Temple or High Priest/Priestess.

Each ritual segment averages 30 minutes in length, with some practices being longer or shorter. Generally the arc of a meeting moves from creating sacred space or banishing, through a formal round of introductions, then into bodywork or spellcraft/results magick, slowly building towards a final main ceremony, which is sacramental or celebratory in nature. Typically breaks can be programmed into this running order to allow periods for practices to settle, visits to the toilet, and cups of tea to be had. This modular structure also means that members of the group can opt in or out of certain practices, leave the session when they need to, and others can arrive later and be included in the narrative of that meeting's process.

So here's a little sample of what we got up to at our recent Equinox meeting. The italicised text is from the notes presented by some of the contributors.

Into the labyrinth...

Hail the September Equinox! Time of balance all across the earth! The clear skies of early autumn provoke the steel-sharp points of stars. The rivers are in full flood; the ocean rises high and drops away.

In the blue there are no boundaries, we recognise this time of balance in the sign of the scales, and we slip, in this northern hemisphere, into the dark.

Together we meet in the garden temple, greeting each other, toasting our company and the spirits of the land and the time. We propitiate Neptune, God of the deep blue sea, asking for riches from his Kingdom. We drum and chant barbarous words. We seal the spell with blue magicians' flash paper.

We recognise the blue of our Buddha nature and of action and reaction. *"The intent behind this ritual is to celebrate and to reaffirm our connections to each other, which are the real source of wealth, to the world, and to the cosmos. The pathway is visualisation - generating blue chaospheres from the throat chakra into the centre..."*

Cut-up excerpt from Derek Jarman's *Blue* (used as a reading to support a tantric practice):

Blue come forth
Blue arise
Blue ascend

Blue come in
Blue protects white from innocence
Blue drags black with it
Blue is darkness made visible
Blue protects white from innocence
Blue drags black with it
Blue is darkness made visible
I have walked behind the sky.
For what are you seeking?
The fathomless blue of Bliss.

We honour the goddess Metis, Goddess of practical wisdom and magical craft. We speak with her in tongues, finding a way between the deep bass rumble of language and the shrill staccato of speech.

Next up is the Arachnoid Apophenia Genogram Rite. *Using the genogram to map our personal family systems so as to more fully appreciate meaningful connection - by adding in other factors - hobbies, pets, fetishes, gods etc, we sought to map our own personal tree of life. Once we had done this we identified one relationship that we wished to transform and sought to use colour, rune staves etc to help focus our intent. We used some trance drumming to aid this process!*

A turquoise magick fills us during the next ceremony. Blue magick filtered through Green, helping us to gain wealth through doing what we love. Making good gold. We pray to Ganesh to break down the obstacles that keep our hearts closed, and to let our love call forth the wealth from our lives.

As night falls another witch woman leads a ritual; *we can follow the descent of the goddess, of Ishtar and Persephone, we can make the quest of the hero with Orpheus, Theseus and Arthur. If we journey into the labyrinth, we can connect to our subconscious, and embrace the coming dark, instead of fighting it.*

All who are willing to explore the spiral path, know this, it is full of mysteries, the labyrinthine ways are shifting, and unsettling, and not for the faint hearted. So we will take the witches' cords with us for protection - the symbol of Ariadne the Goddess of the red thread, which ties us to life, to this world, to reality and sanity.

This thread was enchanted by She who Spins, by She who Measures and by She who Cuts. When I give it to you DO NOT LET GO. Form up the gates, and begin the chant into the labyrinth. Feel the walls growing around you, feel the thread that will lead us home, feel the narrow spiral path leading us down, into the spiral, into the silence, into the shadows. Sink Down, Sink Down, deeper and ever more deep, into eternal and primordial sleep Sink Down, be still, forget and draw apart, into the earth's most secret heart.

Round one spiral, into the core, and out again, we return from this iteration of our descent into the labyrinth.

We move for the final ritual down into the subterranean temple and into The Blue Room.

In the underground circle we give our attention, beginning at the East, to the eight directions and the eight colours. Asking for the wealth of all these forces, we bid them hail and welcome.

Through the gentle equipoise yoga we find our own centre, our point of balance. Poised between the in-breath and the out, between dark and light, heaven and earth.

Blue cords are prepared, and in the centre of the temple a cauldron of rich soil. Cornucopias rest within it, spraying out flowers and seeded stems of the season. A blue ribbon encircles the cauldron and a spiral light of electric blue coils inwards. At its heart is a blue clay vessel containing a sacrament; blue coloured, peach tasting, effervescent water, upon which float delicate slivers of pure gold.

Bringing our attention to the throat chakra we chant the bija mantra of that powerzone, 'Ham'. And knot our cords, bringing awareness to our wealth and to those things, which we would take with us into the dark time to come. The witches' cone of power is raised, majestic, strong and gentle. We relax, body armour coming off, singing and swaying, knotting and pulling the cords until the High Priest cries 'down!' and we drop the power into the cauldron, into the sacrament.

Azure liquid fizzes at our lips, we drink in the gold.

There is laughter and feasting (and a little more magick later that night and indeed the morning, but that, as they say, is another story...).

The seeds begin to come, the fruits of the year, swollen with the light; the early signs of browning decay are everywhere. Spiders spin their dew-spangled webs across improbably wide gulfs. We conjure for wealth and recognition of our wealth, that we may take this gold from the light half of the year into the west, beneath the dark blue waters. We harvest the experience of the light and wrap it in darkness so it may germinate there as ideas, new possibilities, future magick.

The autumn morning; heavy rain drops from indigo swollen clouds.

Golden leaves spiral through the air, to earth.

JV

Blue Magick Spirit Jar

Giving Thanks

A few weeks ago I was sitting by the sea on the beautiful Devon coast. The day was bright, the sky magnificent blue. Meditating in that classic liminal space (where land and sky and sea meet) I took a breath of the Magical Aire. The traditional short-duration but richly decorated visions followed. Returning to awareness of my Self upon the shore, I was shown (as I was digging the spirit paradigm at that moment, though of course I might equally say 'made up in my head') a simple technique that I'd like to share.

Thanks giving

Magical medicines are such that they are magical not only in themselves (as powerful molecules capable of radically changing consciousness) but also in that they are sacraments because they are deployed in a particular way and under particular circumstances. It's what we as magicians bring to the party, as much as the substances themselves, that matters.

One of the most powerful allies when working with these spirits is the sense of gratitude. We recognise that we are blessed to be able to have these potentially moving, healing, insightful, sometimes difficult and often exquisite experiences. What is important to understand here is that this orientation of gratitude to what is going on is quite genuine. And it's simultaneously true that this attitude is a tactic that we, take-no-prisoners chaos magicians, are quite happy to adopt because it gets us what we want (insight, healing, power etc).

So having come out of my trance I wanted to recognise the sacredness of this experience. To write back into my unconscious my gratitude for the insights granted to me and to pave the way for future experiences of liberation.

Acknowledging the Triple Sangha:

After a powerful moment of ritual (with or without medicines...)

Hold the hands in prayer position on the crown of the head. Bring attention to the lineage of gurus who have allowed you to get to this moment in your own spiritual development. Depending on your style you can imagine the sandals of your guru on your head, and their guru on top of them. A great line of teachers stretching into the sky. You might instead choose to imagine this as a community of Stars above you. All those wise people, cunning folk, shamans, explorers and many others who, now, in the past and in the future, have been engaged with the philosophies and techniques of magick. There may be particular teachers, living or dead, that you want to bring your attention to in this moment. This act recognises that we are part of the sangha of these practitioners, in all their myriad forms and traditions.

Next, move the hands in prayer down so that the thumbs press on the Ajna chakra. With this movement bring attention to yourself. You may think of this as the unique and indivisible diamond Atman of your existence. Or you may imagine the self as being the confluence of many forces, acting in the past, present and future. You might wish to pay attention to yourself as a 'conspiracy of selves' or to recognise your own unique narrative (or a combination of all of these interpretations of the Self). In this moment we pay homage to us - our individuality and sense of identity.

Finally the hands are held in prayer at the heart. Bring attention to those beings that support you. Those who love and care for us, who feed and nurture us. This could include humans and other creatures we love, what we eat, the air we breathe and even people and situations we find difficult. However the key focus here is on the sense of being loved and cared for. This is a moment for appreciating those aspects of the universe that provide us with this sense of being valued.

For some rites this act of giving thanks does the same job as the traditional banishing ritual. The usual rules apply. Having spent as long as you need to with this practice go and do something else. Let your awareness of acknowledging these blessings fade into the background reality of your daily life.

JV

Feeding the Spirits

Why worry? The simple answer is that's one of the main things your biology is geared up to do. Humans, in common with probably all other creatures, are designed to worry. It makes biological sense; we need to remember when bad things happen (you eat a poisonous berry, get ambushed by a tiger or whatever) in order to avoid them next time round. Our memory for bad things is phenomenal.

I was teaching mindfulness meditation recently and doing a practice known as the body scan (in which we bring our attention to different parts of our body in order to become mindful of the sensations arising in what can sometimes appear to be the 'separate' vehicle of our bodies). One mediator told me after the session that she had experienced a 'memory' of a neurological problem she'd had with her arm several years before when bringing awareness to that part of her body. She'd not thought about the ailment for many years but, during the body scan, she could feel as if (as Spare might say) the condition had returned. After the session her arm felt perfectly normal but this was a neat insight into how we remember bad stuff and can, under the right conditions, easily recall discomfort, pain and fear.

Of course it's also true to say that humans (and indeed other beasts) are pretty good at normalising things too. Boredom comes naturally to us. Just another day in the gulag, just another abusive email from the regular troll at your website, just another homeless person on the street as you walk to work - even the nastiest things can become humdrum. When the scary becomes predictable then the shock is gone and we slip into dull resignation or even disdain. And that's where worry comes in. If we worry our minds search around for 'the problem'. The curious thing is once 'the problem' is dealt with another new problem arises. Just like the thoughts we encounter in mindfulness. Worrying trains of thought that can be particularly tricky to wake up from because they lock into much of what we, as biological organisms, are meant to do. To recall what was bad, to anticipate future bad stuff, imagining strategies to avoid it in the future. Worry keeps 'the problem' fresh by picking at the scab of attention. And of course, once 'the problem' is solved another problem inevitably arises into awareness.

Should I worry about this...?!

Much of our culture feeds and indeed exacerbates these tendencies in our biology. Much of the media is based on selling fear. Fear, which we gobble up because we like it, our neurology craves it. And to stop our mental palate getting jaded we need that fear to come in a variety of ever morphing forms; terrorism was last week's worry, this week it's phenylbutazone in our horse burgers, next week (after a brief topping up our Middle Eastern crisis levels) perhaps it will be the antics of doomsday cultists or the catastrophic failure of our antibiotic medicines?

This focus on fear surrounds itself with a variety of supporting memes that help us rationalise why we feed ourselves this diet. One such meme is 'realism'; that is, if we don't choose to engage in feeding ourselves this material we must be sticking our heads in the sand, ignoring what's going on in the 'real world' (as though that's what the media presents) and living in a rose-tinted fantasy land. Such a belief can be challenged in a variety of ways. One is the observation that people who choose to engage with lots of mainstream media content, soap operas and so forth are (objectively) less good at assessing risk than those who don't. If you spend your evenings watching gritty hospital dramas and real-life police action shows, you are very likely to hugely overestimate your chances of being involved in a violent crime, and to guess a very high figure for how many people actually die in tragic accidents.

Now I'm not suggesting that we shouldn't be prepared to meet the full horror of the world head on. A visit to the Holocaust galleries of The Imperial War Museum, London is one way to do this or simply dip into the darker side of YouTube (such as the deeply distressing Pathé news film of troops attacking Borneo). It's a necessary condition of an intelligent engagement with the world to consider the destruction of the biosphere, the social inequalities in the world and our own personal pain. But in my view the wise person, the skilled magician, also ensures that their soul is well nourished with delight, compassion and indeed ecstasy.

One process for doing this is the traditional peyote ceremony. The basic technique is to spend a night sitting around a ceremonial fire having ingested the Grandfather medicine. At various points in the vigil the glowing ashes of the central fire are swept out to form the shape of the thunderbird or love heart. Prayer and songs are used to invoke happiness and to promote a sense of thankfulness. Cedar incense is offered to bring purification, and at the end of the rite there is a feast. Grateful of the well-being which the medicine brings, and the support of our Brothers and Sisters around us, in a space of acceptance and respect, joy pushes out the sadness, the worry, the fear. (In some versions there is also a space made for us to admit our faults into this supportive space so that the medicine can do its alchemy). The medicine ceremony grants ecstasy and in that space the healing power of compassion and gratitude may do its work.

From the ashes...

Like mindfulness the ritual of the peyote circle may not change our actual circumstances. But what it can do is provide us with a new input of intense happiness. In the morning our concerns are not magically fixed but what we do have is a space. Worry has been placed in perspective, into a broader context. A little of the free floating anxiety in our lives has passed from the amygdala to the hippocampus and we are better able to face the future from a place that isn't just informed by the gloomier fixations of our simian biology.

There are many ceremonies, many acts, many ways of thinking that we can use to intelligently re-engineer our minds. And while we may face hard times, to do so from a place of equipoise is much more likely to lead to accurate judgement of situations and good choices than if our minds are full of fear. We're also much more likely to be capable of experiencing and indeed creating happiness for others and ourselves.

So with whatever ways are at your disposal, feed your soul and may you be able to discover the delight in your life in the past, present and the future.

JV

Still Curious

I can't help myself, I've been thinking about doubt again! Reading over some of the posts on this blog I started getting a bit anxious about all the uncertainty that our hip postmodernism seems to be embodying. If faith based belief systems seem inaccessible to us, what as a magician do I do in order to prevent a descent into madness?

In my day job as a psychological therapist, I was recently reading a great article by the systemic psychotherapist Barry Mason. In it he maps out the shift in his understanding of how certain he felt he could be in his work with families and asks the question "is uncertainty mainly a path to creativity or a path to paralysis?"

As he grapples with this question, he outlines three types of knowing; unsafe certainty (based on outdated or inaccurate assumptions), unsafe uncertainty (one's environment provides neither safety nor coherent beliefs), and finally safe uncertainty. Safe uncertainty exists when one's environment and strategies for managing life allows for uncertainty to be lived with and even embraced.

Now I like this a lot; in my own journey I have experienced faith-based certainty which gave a period of respite. For me it provided a warm fog that protected me from much of life's sharpness. As I have previously, I felt a genuine grief when I had to walk away from certainties that were no longer congruent with my experience of reality. My certainty was no longer safe.

Mason talks about the need to cultivate curiosity and seeks to frame the therapist's role as being one of an explorer who seeks to embody "authoritative doubt".

Magicians are generally those interested in exploring the terrain of the psyche and body rather than rushing toward union with the divine. Curiosity, experimentation and reflection create an interactive process where the Self becomes a lab from which working hypotheses can be derived and refined. Such reflective experiments can be wide in their parameters and address the big issues of our sex lives, the food that we eat and what we think about death.

I have to confess, my problem with believing in things has followed me on my journey. I am a half-hearted Thelemite and a piss-poor pagan. Crowley both annoys and inspires me and I find most polytheistic theologies inane. What I have always been drawn to are those outsider Gods of consciousness. These are the Magician Gods that embody the archetype of the individual who is seeking to wake up. Shiva, Odin, Set, Sekhmet, Mercury; truth seekers who themselves are wrestling with the mysteries of the universe. Wisdom and power are hard won for these Gods - eyes are sacrificed, brothers are killed, and periods of celibacy are embraced. It's this type of consciousness or awareness that I am seeking.

In the face of not knowing, I can still step up and exercise some existential heroism. As a magician I chose myself as the locus of my Work and attention. I may need a school or good friends to check my narcissism, but as a magician I have given up pleasing Gods; I will start with transforming myself. If they happen to like this Promethean wilfulness, good for them! This act of Becoming is my expression of the law of Thelema. While I have it, I choose to revel in this gift of consciousness.

This focus on becoming, and the discovery of Will, has not been an act of teeth gritting and über-humanity; one of my primary goals has also been the cultivation of receptivity. In and through a greater awareness of the space between things, the life force (Kia, Tao etc.) can then flow. This is less a magic of enforced will, more an exercise in observing where the fault-lines of probability are and then enhancing them.

Cultivating an awareness of possibilities

Coming back then to my initial question of how to minimize my impending breakdown, I choose to act. Paradoxically this also entails the action of non-action -sitting with, and accepting, the limits of what can be currently known. My own personal praxis centres on the use of approaches that at once develop Will and also help me sit with mystery and not knowing. Still curious, still exploring.

SD

Black
The Darkness of Hallowe'en

Black water covers the earth, seeping down into the cracks, sliding into the hidden places.

Hallowe'en, Samhain, in the direction of Northwest on the wheel of the year, is a time of Black Magick.

We sat around the kitchen table, one Sister unable to join us because of the flooding, and played an esoteric parlour game. The challenge; write down a list of your top 13 deities. Having done so we can compare lists and make those knowing noises that one makes during a divination. Our selections are similar, with some deities being shared across a number of personal pantheons. Then another game; write down the first three words you associate with the phrase 'Left-hand Path' - more light-hearted but valuable insights into our group process.

We meet by the fireside. Banishing the space with the Gnostic Chaosphere Ritual (version 1.8, see *The Book of Baphomet*), we make toasts to absent friends, and the spirits and powers of the time. The first Work is the Black Mage hibernation rite.

The Black Mage magical hibernation rite: This working has been inspired by Michael Kelly's writing on the Black Mage in Apophis and my own thinking on 'Slow Magick'. The Black Mage for me resonates with the fecund earth and the unconscious, the primal rune Uruz and the Muladhara chakra. When we are able to work with the energy of the Black Mage we will hopefully access our unique primal power. The aim of this ritual is to loosen our bodily conditioning and then direct both power and intent toward planting a desired outcome into the dark part of the year.

Method: Opening with singing bowl, group breath work followed by 5 minutes dancing/seething to the track "Geneva" by Russian Circles (chosen because of its dark, overwhelming heaviness!). Once our body armour has been loosened via movement, we adopt the yogic asana "pose of a child" and groan the rune Uruz into the ground (x8) - thus planting our "slow" magic into the turning of the year. Close with prayer of thanksgiving and reflection.

For the next ritual we descend into the subterranean temple. This is work in defence of the ash trees in Europe which are threatened by a newly emerging disease. This ritual is the brilliant 'Activating the Glass Harp Virus Smasher'.

"This is the water that will heal the land,
This is the water that will create sound,
This is the water that will create form..."

Next our Sister leads a meditation. This is the Vision of
Sorrow in Binah, framed by the symbolism of the four 3s from
the tarot; The Three of Disks - Work, The Three of Cups -
Abundance, The Three of Wands - Virtue, The Three of
Swords - Sorrow. Cards placed in each quarter, we spend time
sitting with these concepts. For my part I go through in my
mind all the people I know and love, I say their name silently
and acknowledge that they 'will die'. I acknowledge the death
of my children, my parents, my lovers, my colleagues and
many more. And strangely as I follow the truth and constancy
of death in all these lives I realise that it's okay, the muscles in
my face lift and I find that, by the end of our practice, I'm
smiling. We're all going to die, and that's okay. We're all equal
and I feel compassion, equanimity and even joy in that shared
commonality.

The next Work is my offering. Once more underground, I have
prepared a pentacle upon which smokes an incense of rich,
sticky gums and the earthy scent of patchouli. Lying down, the
travellers in the vision are wrapped in blankets and a stone is
placed upon each of their chests. This gentle pressure is their
anchor as they travel backwards into deep time, into the
moment of The Fall of Because - the mysterious imagined
time where our species became estranged from the 'natural
order'. Each traveller holds a pearl. The physical anchor for
the intention to transform the Fall into something else, to
transform it with hope, with magick. As the members of our
circle inhale this sacred smoke and settle back to journey, I
switch on a track that mixes trance drumming with the
Shepard Tone, and I tell them the story;

Think of all the problems in the world, war, species
collapse, human generated climate change, mindless drone
jobs, the surveillance state, nuclear catastrophe, resource
scarcity, famine, population pressures, violence, abuse, fear,

pollution, slavery, rapacious capitalism that is literally, exponentially, eating the world...

Think of all the reasons why we might be in this state, technological processes, poor communication, alpha male dominator culture, writing, domestication, capitalism, democracy - why are we like this, how is it that we, humanity, are fallen?

Think of all the religions and the belief systems of the ages, who have tried to grapple with the problems of human nature, with their instructions for how to live, how to die, their ideas of suffering, of sin, of apocalypse, and perhaps revelation and redemption.

Think how many belief systems posit a golden age, a time in Eden, a time before we were separated from God. Before this Kali Yuga, before we were lost.

Think back now, back into history, our story.

Think back to the days of Victorian era, the age of our Empire, colonial expansion, of the wild piratical early modern period, back to the medieval age of knights and castles, back to the ancient world; those earliest of civilisations - the Sumerians, the Maya, all the way back to the first cities to Çatalhöyük, to Göbekli Tepe, and before...

Back now further, back to those earliest of farmers, the first domesticated grains, the first domesticated animals, the first domesticated humans. The first State that counted production, enclosed fields, numbered the biological and controlled it with technology. And back further still, into deep time, into the world of our ancestors before we began to farm. Back to those hunter-gatherer communities, running through the forest with the deer. Back to the first fires, the first stories, back to the first words.

And back further still to the Nameless Wordless Aeons before our awareness arose, before the collapse into Nature and Culture, before our Fall.

Now from this deep timeline find the moment for you; that period in history, or prehistory, in the journey of our species, where you place the Fall, the 'Because' that determines our sense of separation into Civilisation and the uncivilised, nature versus culture, wild verses tame... that moment of the fall.

And there, in that moment place your seed pearl, your intention, and your hope in Pandora's box. That glyph of the uniting of Self and Other, nature and culture, without Because and into doing. Place that bright hope into the moment of the fall so that by which we fall, we also rise, and we may fall no more.

Returning immediately, breaking into the Now our travellers are back. Knowing that The Fall has never happened. The chest stones are set aside, the pearls cast into a vessel of black water. We are each anointed with red-brown ochre, symbol of renewed life from the depths of the earth. In celebration of this we sing together:

We are ancient
As ancient as the sun
We came from the ocean
Once our ancestral home
So that one day
We could all return
To our birthright
The great celestial dome
We are the children of the sun
Our journey's just begun
Sunflowers in our hair
We are the children of the sun

There is room for everyone
Sunflowers in our hair

Children of the Sun by Dead Can Dance

Finally for this night, our Brother sets up a little Mexican Day of the Dead shrine in the centre of the temple. Peering into that tiny glass box, he reads a poem he has written. This reminds me of something I wrote about a Hallowe'en over a decade ago in *Now That's What I Call Chaos Magick* about the beauty and power of simply listening, with right-attention, to inspirational text.

Later one of our Brothers drives home. At one point his way is barred by black, fast flowing water. He abandons his car and wades his way across the flood-land delighting in the wildness of the experience.

In the morning the deluge of the night has broken into bands of rain punctuated by brilliant sunshine. My Brother and I watch Alejandro Jodorowski's *The Holy Mountain* and go for a walk out on the salt-marsh. The earth squeaks its water-logged fullness, a rapid river, spotted with bobbing dead wood, is bound for the sea.

The following night I gather the leftover materials from our magick into a spirit jar; ashes, red wine, black water, pearls. Whereas the spirit house for Blue Magic shines with azure stones, blue spell cords and flecks of gold, this Black Magic vessel is full of a dark liquid in which are hidden five nacreous gems of hope.

JV

The Waters of Return

Beelzebub Speaks...

One of the very cool things that the Temple of Set has turned me on to (especially the Esoteric Order of Beelzebub) are the great insights that can be gained by an initiate in more fully appreciating the Gurdjieff Work. The Temple employs numerous ways for seeking to actualize the Self, but the framework offered by the Fourth Way teachings of Gurdjieff and his followers provides a nuanced language for the pursuit of awakening within daily life.

Even a cursory glance at either Gurdjieff's own writing or that of Ouspensky (cf. *In Search of the Miraculous*) will demonstrate the complexity of the teachings both in terms of their cosmology and ontology. With its deliberate obscuration, coined phrases and frankly bonkers pseudo-gnostic mythos, the Work provides us with a set of ideas that are as intriguing and infuriating as the twilight language of Tantra.

In short, the Work views humanity's normal state of being as machine-like. The demands of culture, family, our bodies and our lives have made us automatons. We are on autopilot, we are asleep. The aim of the Work is wake us from this sleep. The existence of our soul cannot be presumed upon, it must be worked for, and fought for - Soul must be created. But how is one to accomplish such a task?

Gurdjieff recognised that throughout humanity's' history we have sought to connect to God/HGA/True Self etc. He believed that these efforts could be typified via the centre or starting point from which The Seeker began their journey. In short, these paths are the way of the body (the fakir), the way of the heart (the monk) and the way of the mind (the yogi). Whatever benefit may have been gained in the past through the pursuit of these means, in our age and within a life lived outside of monastery walls, we need something more. For Gurdjieff this is the Fourth Way.

Gurdjieff - bald, piercing eyes, what's not to like?

The Fourth Way is the way of "the cunning man" - the one who seeks to harmonize body, heart and mind as they seek to awaken solar consciousness. The Work challenges us to Self-remember, to become more awake within the bodymind. The methods we may employ, like Beelzebub, are legion, but the goal of seeking soulful awakened depth remains.

Folks like me who are into postmodern magic are always banging on about "the map is not the territory". But we still need maps. Frankly, if lost I'd rather make use of a sketchy map than none at all. Now maps can always be improved upon, and there is the danger that we spend so much time looking at the bloody map that we miss the incoming weather front.... Maps hopefully provide us with a sense of where we are in the landscape and where we need to travel in order to reach our destination.

Magic without a teleological goal can easily descend into what Chogyam Trungpa called "spiritual materialism". Without some general sense of direction, we can end up endlessly turning in circles, covering the same territory and end up feeling completely exhausted (sound familiar?). The Work potentially provides us with a helpful (if at times eccentric) map for avoiding such a pitfall.

Personally, the Gurdjieff Work provides me with a more 'Western', hermetic take on my mindfulness practice. This Zen Odinist doesn't have to retreat and seek a rarefied atmosphere to awaken; the way of the cunning man lays open before me now. My current spiritual preoccupations may lead me to focusing on a particular Centre or "Way", but the other paths act as challenging voices asking to me to come back to that liminal place where I can walk the knife-edge.

The sleeper must Awaken.

SD

Death of a Chaos Magician

Magicians are generally those interested in exploring the terrain of the psyche and body rather than rushing toward union with the divine. Experimentation and reflection create an interactive process where the Self becomes a lab from which working hypotheses can be derived and refined. Such reflection can be about our sex life, the food that we eat or what we think about death. Death used to hold no fear for me.

Certainty provided me with a set of blinkers that blocked off the messy realities of a world that didn't fit my faith. That faith (a Christian one) is now long gone but the tenets of the Nicene Creed are not the only victims. The death of that identity came via a very painful existential crisis that nearly cost me my mind. From the furnace of that testing I came face-to-face with a realisation about myself: I could no longer allow myself the comfort that belief claimed to offer. I was on the hunt for gnosis.

Hunting for gnosis

The search that compelled me to seek means for shifting consciousness eventually brought me to the door of Chaos Magic. Its heady melange of anarchic creativity and punk rock pragmatism sought to give the rather stuffy halls of Western magic a good spring-clean. Undue reverence was no longer given to a batch of half-baked theosophical dogmas as the new magi sought to grapple with the joys of fuzzy logic and Post-Structuralism.

Generally I feel that such a paradigm shift has been positive, and yet after working with this approach for well over a decade I began to feel troubled. I began to wonder whether its over-referenced hipness and self-conscious flippancy provided answers to what it truly means to live and die as a magician. If I can no longer cling to certainty with regards the Summerland, or some mapped out process of rebirth, could Current 23 help me deal with the big questions?

In his excellent *Prime Chaos* Phil Hine contrasts two of the primary paradigms with which the chaos tradition has played: Discordianism and the Cthulhu Mythos. Discordianism (or Liber Nice as Phil calls it) represents the irreverent, playful face of Chaos Magic. Inspired by anarchist Situationism, the spirit of Eris invites us to joyfully embrace the absurdity of both life and death. Our attempts to control and predict are laughed at by the non-linear nature of realities. Now when faced by the loss of those people, things and ideas dearest to us, laughing may not be on the agenda. Yet the holy fool of Discordianism encourages us to half-smile into the face of grief and to hold on to things with an open handed lightness. I would highly recommend the video interviews that Robert Anton Wilson did as his own death approached - one can't help but be moved by the sense of spaciousness and compassion that are palpable as he struggles with his pain and impending departure. Hail Eris! Hail RAW!

Ia! Ia! Cthulhu Ftagn! The Cthulhu mythos (Liber Nasty!) presents us with unredeemable vision of cosmic horror. In his seminal *Liber Koth*, Stephen Sennitt maps out an eight spoked pathworking via which the Adept can engage with these dark denizens. Azathoth, Nyarlathotep and their colleagues inhabit a qliphotic realm of dark, really dark and pitch black. To work with the Mythos means engaging with such hazardous realms and the sense of psychic compression that such adventures bring.

Ia! Ia!

Why do we like this stuff? It's like a cosmic car crash that we can't look away from, but does it have significance beyond our fetish for heavy metal aesthetics? For me the world of Lovecraft embodies our sense of horror in response to the Universe's vast uncertainty. The monster-gods of the mythos provide us with a potent set of shadow archetypes that can be sat with and glanced at sideways. This is not easy work, but if handled wisely the Mythos gives us a vehicle via which we can channel our all too real terror of death and non-existence.

Ecstasy as rehearsal:

One of the most positive aspects of Chaos Magic as a style of working has been its emphasis on the Dionysian. The state of trance, whether this be of ecstasy/excitation or inhibition, has been one of the primary technologies that it utilises as a tradition.

Its forefather Austin Osman Spare was critical in rescuing the Magical tradition from a dusty and over-linear style of working. His work stressed the use of the non-linear and the unconscious. The use of sigils, automatic writing/drawing and the death posture all ask us to let go of our attempts to control. The lust for results must be swamped by the dark flow of Kia.

Much has been made in contemporary shamanisms about the role of initiatory death and dismemberment - the Shaman is destroyed by the realm of the Spirits so as to be remade. Such may also be the experience of the Chaos Magician. Whatever remanifestation our selves will take when our physical body conks out; the states of ecstasy sought by the work of magic provide us with a dress rehearsal. The type of belief-shifting that the Chaotic approach employs often leads to a sense of loss, disorientation and jarring weirdness. Too much of this will lead to psychic burnout, but more judicious application can be both entertaining and informative. This approach, with the potential uncertainty that it creates, can feel like a little death for the psyche - arguably good practice for what's ahead.

So does this leave us stuck in some trendy but ultimately futile spiritual dead-end street (pun intended)? Hopefully not. If we are able to ride the currents of the zeitgeist in such a way as to open up greater freedom and possibility, then Chaos Magic may help us in developing inner poise. This is not the certainty of faith, but a sense of knowing based on practice.

Yogis, mystics and sages have spent millennia experimenting with the Self. What can we learn for ourselves about life and death if we follow a similar path?

What's ahead?

My own journey continues to be an exercise in developing curiosity. If I work with these states of ecstasy and the expansion of Self that they represent, where am I left in facing the ultimate mystery of death? I find myself in a place of openness - sitting with my own uncertainty and fear, but also open to the possibility of a further becoming and remanifestation that even the Vale of Death cannot contain.

SD

Black Magick and Shooting Rabbits

Shooting rabbits isn't easy. At least that's what a friend of mine has discovered recently. The Devonian farmhouse in which he lives boasts a magnificent garden with a pond, numerous fruit trees and a large lawn. In the evening, while reading in his library, my friend could see rabbits emerge from the hedges and begin to feed. As a confirmed gourmet he decided that a stew with rabbit harvested from his own land would be something to have a go at. With this in mind he purchased an air gun.

The next day the rabbits were back, nibbling the grass and burrowing under the apple tree roots and damaging them in the process. My friend left the library to obtain the weapon but upon his return the rabbits had, miraculously it seemed, vanished.

Prince of a Thousand enemies

This went on for some time. Occasionally he would get as far as opening the library door, gun in hand, before his quarry would disappear. Yet other times they seemed to be sensitive to his murderous intentions before he was even able to open the door. What was going on? Did the rabbits possess some remarkable psychic power? Some precognitive skill that was able to preserve them from the hunter?

Finally my friend was successful in bagging himself a bunny. He'd figured out what was going on and adapted his behaviour in such a way that the rabbits were no longer disturbed by his armed presence. However having killed one animal it's now the case that the rabbits are steering clear of the lawn (at least during twilight).

So what was going on in this situation? As anyone who has hunted will tell you, when we attempt to stalk an animal it's not only the quarry we need to watch out for. In this case, even while in his library, the movement of my friend, especially the type of movement he was making (to get his gun and quietly try to slip out the French windows) was alerting the whole network of relationships in the garden. Birds notice what's going on and give their alarm calls. This alerts the rabbits, which take cover.

This reminds me of a point made by a psychedelics researcher during his lecture at the recent academic conference concerning psychedelics, *Breaking Convention*. In trying to explain the expanded sense of awareness that the drug NMT creates he quoted a remark made to him by an aboriginal elder. The elder asked, 'How can you know if something is coming, even if it's kilometres away from where you are?' The answer is to listen deeply, to attune the hearing down to the level of the murmur of insects in the landscape. As the object or animal approaching perturbs these buzzings and chirrupings and flappings, so those changes cascade through the reptiles, the birds and the mammals in the landscape. Alarm calls are issued by many species and so the clever listener can hear that something is coming long before the noise of the object itself is discernible.

What happens in the bush is identical to what happens in the Devon countryside. The rabbits were listening not just to my friend attempting to sneak up on them with his gun. Their senses were attuned to the background hum that life forms in that landscape. In this way they appeared to have miraculous powers of perception.

It's easy for us humans, with our amazing ability to focus on just one thing amid a range of inputs, to forget about this kind of background, holistic perception. Yet this effect goes on around us all the time. When we enter a situation there are the bits of it (people, objects, products, events) upon which we are focussed and then there are all those intimately interconnected elements that we may disregard as irrelevant. But if we want to successfully engage with the subject of our intervention (i.e. to shoot the rabbit) we must bear these things in mind.

In magick, as in hunting, similar rules apply. For instance, we might want to explore or change some aspect of ourselves, or indeed the world around us, by our practices. As we attempt to do so we may discover that our 'quarry' is intimately bound-up with other aspects of the self or wider universe. We may then discover that we can't go straight from A to B but have to spend some time settling into a new pattern, gently putting things 'at their ease' before we progress.

This is particularly important in cultures like ours that often emphasise the importance of speedy results and goal orientated behaviours. One might for example contrast the permaculture approach to land management with that of industrialised farming. The ideal permaculture way of working with a given area of land is to spend at least a year simply observing it. Finding out how it works, talking to people who have known the land over time, spending time in and among the beings that populate the space. After a time of observation, the logic runs, what we decide to grow, to build and to change about the land in question, can be informed by our active observations and growing sensitivity to that particular place. The contrast with the quick, results driven approach of industrialised farming, where land is not much more than raw space for activity, is a dramatic one.

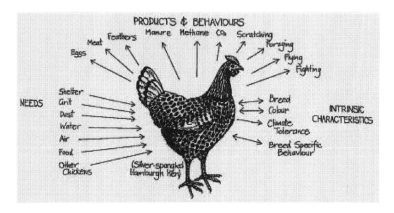

Permaculture chicken

Given these facts it's not surprising that the beginner in magick often fails to take their time, and it's true that even experienced adepts sometimes find themselves being too quick to focus on 'the result' they are after. Not only can this mean we miss the delight of the journey to our goal, but, as with the case of the rabbits, our thundering presence in the woodland of the unconscious can spook our target and leave us none the wiser about why things went wrong.

When we talk of magick it's easy to imagine that we're talking about what Starhawk defined as 'power-over'. Being in control, being the ruler of the psyche - all sigils and kick-ass cere-monies and servitors an' shit. Whereas, as the skilled hunter knows (be they a rabbit hunter or the kid waiting motionless by the rock pool, eager to see the slow gyrations of water snails), there is great power in stealth, in silence and in sensitivity. All those barbaric words are pretty cool, but they're not going to work too well unless we know how to listen.

This sensitivity, one might conjecture, is more likely to lead to an intelligent view of the world as an interconnected whole. It may also lead to moral qualities such as the pursuit of virtue, compassion and tolerance. Beyond this it could be the basis for a holistic perception of the world that transcends the narrow confines of the assumed self but does not abandon the reality of our individual narrative (one could say (True) Will) in the world. In a sense this is 'black magick' in that it's focused around getting what we want (in this case, some excellent rabbit stew) but in order to get what we want we find ourselves developing our sensitivity to the universe; expanding our notion of who we are, and better understanding our story, and that of others.

JV

Orders, Disorders and doing the Great Work

One of the books that I keep coming back to over the years of exploration is Ouspensky's *In Search of the Miraculous*. Now, anyone who has had a go at engaging with this book's densely typed 400 pages knows that it is hardly easy reading. Not only do we have Ouspensky's own vivid struggle to develop a relationship with his teacher/anti-hero G.I. Gurdjieff, but we also have to wrestle with the detailed explanation/obscuration of their rather 'out there' Gnostic cosmology.

Part of the reason that I keep returning both to this challenging tome, and the Fourth Way teachings that it describes, is the way in which they seek to grapple with the nature of what awakening might mean and also how we do this collectively. I have already written on this blog about my take on the Fourth Way work's depiction of how the "Sly Man" seeks to actualize body, mind and emotions and thought it would be helpful to reflect on Gurdjieff's perspective on the importance of collective endeavour.

A Sly Man having a crafty drink.

As in most things Gurdjieff is refreshingly unapologetic in insisting on the importance of needing to have a "school" or group in order to make real progress in esoteric work:

> "The point is that a "group" is the beginning of everything. One man can do nothing, can attain nothing. A group with a real leader can do more. A group of people can do what one man can never do." Pg. 30.

For Gurdjieff, the School provided an essential reflective environment in which the spiritual progress of an individual could be plotted against a more impersonal/transpersonal measure. Whatever the benefits of close personal friendship and its value in enriching our lives, the concept of the school or Order ideally provides a context where the "work" of initiatory endeavour can be framed by principles and boundaries that hope to minimize the unpredictability of whimsy and clashes of ego.

For many this will sound like a pipedream and such idealisation raises real concerns about the potential misuses of hierarchy and authority. In recent decades many magical practitioners have wanted to challenge the received wisdom concerning the necessity and desirability of needing such pyramidal structures. Some argue that they play into our consumerist tendency to quantify advancement in terms of elaborate titles and the acquisition of magical bling. In trying to evolve different approaches, people have begun to seek looser, more tribal arrangements that aim to encourage growth and fraternity while avoiding the "stuckness" that can plague minority orthodoxies and magical hegemonies.

Recent discussions with friends regarding these dilemmas have considered the potential contrast between the qabalistically informed hierarchy of "Freemasonic" structures and the more "flattened" polyarchical dynamics of Rosicrucian fraternities. As someone who currently belongs to both a formal magical order and a number of more informal working collectives, I felt that I'd share some of what I consider to be the potential benefits and pitfalls of both models.

Personally speaking, being part of a more formal magical Order has provided me with an excellent opportunity to learn. While undertaking any deep spiritual work will inevitably lead to the forming of close relationships with others, one of the strengths of an order is that they usually have a solid corpus of techniques and perspectives to engage with. Even if I might not agree with some of what's being proposed, the content and structure of such systems provide me with something solid to bash up against and thus refine my own initiatory understanding. The pursuit of grades and curricula may become yet another form of "spiritual materialism", but at best they can fulfil our need for structure and a way of mapping our development, especially in the early to intermediate stages of training.

Working with others can be tricky. In traditions that involve hermetic, magical or tantric perspectives there is a certain inevitability that we will need to challenge existing values and certainties. While they will never be perfect in their execution, many Orders out of necessity have had to spend time reflecting on how they provide boundaries and guidance to ensure that ethical standards are understood and respected. Such learning often takes decades of shared work to develop maturity. Groups will always make mistakes in the doing of the great work, but what feels critical is that they have mechanisms for feedback and reflection so that the inevitable mistakes are learnt from.

The desire to evolve more informal groupings of practitioners working together is hardly a new impulse. Such sodalities are often the beginnings of many formal orders, and are also the primary modus operandi for many covens and hearths. These smaller 'circles' of practitioners often rely on a fair degree of pre-existing magical competence, and a shared focus on working with a specific theme or group of deities.

What (groups of) witches do...

My own experience is that they can provide a great arena for magical experimentation, but that they inevitably have to manage the issues of who sets the agenda and the necessary grounds for inclusion/ exclusion. It's probable that most groups evolve a basic leadership and initiatory structure in response to emergent dynamics within the life of such groups. Often issues of power and direction need to be brought above ground in order to reduce their disruptive potential should they remain at an unconscious or shadow level. We may wish to work hard in minimising the negative aspects of hierarchy, but equally most of us don't enjoy sailing in a rudderless ship!

Each of us has different learning styles and political sensitivities that will shape the type of magical environment that will be most conducive to our development. We may stick with one style of group process or we may feel the need for necessary diversification or counter-balance. For some, the realities of geographical distance may mean that relationships are primarily reliant on cyber-interactions as a means of deepening engagement. What feels critical to me is that we retain the insight that the Great Work is an act of both doing and connection, which can only be understood in attempting its undertaking and in receiving support and feedback from others. As necessary as our theologies and ideologies might be, their true value only becomes clear when we pressure test them in the forge of praxis, and weigh them according to the extent to which they expand our humanity.

SD

Octarine
Opening as Octarine

Twelfth night. Yule itself, and Christmas too, have come and gone. Family gatherings have happened; we've comforted ourselves in the darkness with rich foods; roasts, figs, chocolate, wine and more.

Yuletide glitz

Now our group turns its attention to the symbolism of Octarine - the colour of magick, the north & midwinter. We gather for these rituals by the hearth of our Covenstead. In the corner of the room the Christmas tree twinkles its little lights. A large reproduction of Atu XV - The Devil, Lord of Misrule and capricious midwinter goat - graces the temple. There are drums and rattles for music (an essential component for our meetings) and the altar glitters with peacock feathers, holly and festive lights.

'The colour of magick that can be described is not the true colour'. Octarine sits outside of our symbolic categorisations; it is beyond what we know and, more directly than the other rays of the chaos star, points towards the ungraspable nature of the Mystery.

We open the temple with the Gnostic Chaosphere Ritual (v01.8), and pass a cup of ginger wine round the circle, which summons a warming, seasonal glow. The first ritual is the 'Octarine Pineal Gland Working'. In this practice we install a homunculus in our brains, a miniature visualisation of ourselves, sat in the core of our brains, massaging our pineal bodies. The internal adept gently rubs the gland and from it the octarine secretions are released, flooding through the whole being. This magickal fluid opens us to the transcendental. Causing the brain to unfold like a flower blooming in the night, unfurling like a receiver to cosmic consciousness.

The Brother leading the ceremony plays the singing bowl and thingshaws, and we sit for a while under the imagined winter stars, bathed in octarine radiance.

In the next rite we conjure 'The Chalice of Becoming'. Our Sister has drawn water from the sacred spring of St. Aldhelm, and this is poured into a silver cup. Using gestures and sounds at each direction, the elements are called. The chalice is carried round the temple as we move to each quarter, the sacred water absorbing the words of power that we speak, quivering in sympathy with the moments we make.

We sit while a singing bowl sounds; meditating on what it is that we need, what we feel the drive to Become. When the meditation is done we each speak our desires aloud into the water, pronouncing our words over the liquid so that it absorbs the vibrations of the sound.

We leave the temple and, in the garden, pour the clear (or is it octarine?) fluid onto the cold, dark earth.

Our next ritual is part of an ongoing series of workings, delicate political magic and not something I can go into too much detail about at present. As Princess Irulan remarks in Frank Herbert's Dune 'A beginning is a very delicate time'. Suffice it to say that 'the colour that must not be named' was summoned to create a bridge between our group and the spirit we want to work with.

The final ceremony of the meeting concerned the impossibility of containing the Mystery. I'd been enjoying the work of an American fundamentalist preacher and considering how all his spiritual knowledge was referenced to the King James Version of the Bible. Understandable but still strange how we seek to limit, to know, to create certainty, even in our dealings with the Mystery, or God or whatever one wants to name it.

Still skyclad from the previous rite, we pulled the powers of the eight directions into our circle. Asking for illumination from each of the eight colours of magick, from the sabbats and energies associated with them.

I wanted to call on the power of perhaps one of the earliest spiritual frames of reference, and to this end, had been researching the Yezidi and their key symbol of The Peacock Angel Tawûsê Melek. The Yezidi religion looks very like an ancient paganism of the Middle East, wrapped in an old wrapper of text and tradition which (arguably) reaches back to the deep time of Göbekli Tepe and Sumer. The lustrous shine of the peacock's tail reminded me of octarine and of course the iridescent transformative stage of alchemy. Then there is the suggestion that the Yezidi (in common with Wiccans and Heathens) hold the north as the most sacred direction of the compass.

We made prayers. These had to be from memory and so for many participants they were those from the Christian tradition, the framework for the sacred that many of us learnt as children.

I then read the words of Tawûsê Melek, as given in the *Kitab al-Jilwa, The Book of Revelation*:

"I lead to the straight path without a revealed book; I direct aright my beloved and my chosen ones by unseen means. All my teachings are easily applicable to all times and all conditions. I punish in another world all who do contrary to my will. Now the sons of Adam do not know the state of things that is to come. For this reason they fall into many errors. The beasts of the earth, the birds of heaven, and the fish of the sea are all under the control of my hands. All treasures and hidden things are known to me; and as I desire, I take them from one and bestow them upon another. I reveal my wonders to those who seek them, and, in due time my miracles to those who receive them from me. But those who are without are my adversaries, hence they oppose me. Nor do they know that such a course is against their own interests, for might, wealth, and riches are in my hand, and I bestow them upon every worthy descendant of Adam. Thus the government of the worlds, the transition of generations, and the changes of their directors are determined by me from the beginning."

Then we sat again in meditation, considering for ourselves the spontaneous, surprising and unlooked for moments in which we had each encountered the Mystery. Moments perhaps arising from ceremony or other spiritual work, but particularly those times where these experiences, of gnosis, of ecstasy, had appeared unbidden. We remember those times when our revelation overturned our expectations and previous beliefs.

The times where the octarine Mystery burst the banks of our paradigm and inundated our reality.

We take a moment to listen for the unstruck sound in the deep midwinter.

Moving from this space. We now open ourselves to the wild delight of Mystery, of the midwinter goat, and dance to the words of a fire-and-brimstone preacher, re-purposed as an invocation to Baphomet. (During numerous rituals we made use of digital technology to create original visual art and music for our Work.) Baphomet is the god who has no myth; the deity without fixed form, the freakish hybrid of unknown possibility - Io Baphomet!

There is food and music and delightful conversation later that night (and another digital cut-up sermon plus dance backing-track, from our favourite pastor, this time testifying about the pineal gland and illumination). The year turns towards the light and, with full bellies, thankful of our riches and curious of the unknown nature of the year ahead, we step into the Mystery.

JV

Breaking open the head

Seeking the Octarine

Why do I do Magick? I'm serious, I've put a lot of effort into this hobby of mine and I think the question is worth asking. Is it simply that I desire more power and toys? Frankly, no. As a Chaos magician, though I might be keen to stress the practical 'results magick' focus of the tradition, this in itself is not enough. For this to be sustainable there has to be something more.

One of the big questions for me as a magician has been concerning this whole issue of teleos, or end game. When arguably "nothing is true", can those of us caught up in the swirling vortex of Postmodern culture speak meaningfully of Meaning? As time goes on I find myself thinking less about the magick that I do and more about the magician that I'm seeking to become. That's not to say that I want to become a mystic who only wants union with Kia/God/the Void - I'm still interested in the terrain of the journey and the techniques of exploration. But Magick without a goal like awakening seems little more than an exotic form of acquisition.

What I'm beginning to suspect is that the transformations that I often strive for in my circumstances, are primarily alchemical changes in myself. The more magick that I do, the more sacrifice that it seems to demand of me, and the more my character becomes the locus of change. So I'm sensing one of those strange loops or circularities - I'm a magician who realises that the more I do magic, the more it's going to cost me. In order to avoid such a price, bizarrely I seem to be acting more skilfully and it's as though the magick has already been done! Now this is weird - is the magician at risk of becoming the magick? What's the relationship between my day-to-day self and the aspirant in the robe?

In *Liber Kaos*, Pete Carroll (peace be upon him) talks about this realm of Magick as being the Octarine or "the eighth power of the self":

> "The growth of the octarine, or eighth power of the self, and the discovery of the type of magician one wants to be, and the identification or synthesis of a god-form to represent it, tend to create something of a mutant being, who has advanced into a paradigm that few others are aware of." (p. 113)

My Magick is causing me to mutate - self-inflicted memetic infection if you will.

This seems to be where sorcery gives way to deeper initiatory work- the tantric goal of not eliminating desire, rather using it as a means of transformation and ongoing self-refinement.

As a big fan of both Vampires and Storm Constantine's Wraeththu mythology I like the idea of mutating. We are becoming something more, something else; not in some steel willed übermensch stylee, but as humans dancing with our potential. We are seeking that state where art meets science - that optimal state of Flow. As magicians we seek to dance with the relativity of time - dreaming of how we might be and invoking our future Selves so that they might whisper in our ears.

Potent kinetic energy

For me then, the focus of my current work is less about fixating about who this future self might be; rather I seek to use my spiritual practice to cultivate the type of attentiveness that will help me remain open to the possibilities. Let's keep dancing!

SD

Spirals

Sometimes I feel like I'm going around in circles. As part of my day job as a therapist, it feels that part of my raison d'être is witnessing the strange spirals in the lives of other human beings. For those who think that change happens in a straight line, they probably haven't been paying attention in class. Whether it's related to addictions work, relationship difficulties or trying to more skilfully manage emotions, most of us have to revisit what the pros call "the cycle of change" at least several times before things shift.

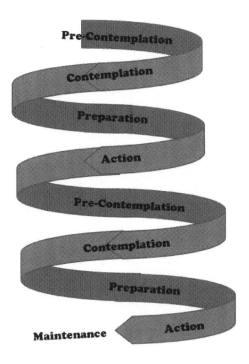

Spirals of change

The cycle of change (cf. the work of Prochaska and DiClemente) recognises that for most of us, for the act of changing to be sustainable usually involves contemplation (thinking about how it might be different) and preparation before we actually "do" something behaviourally. Now this is all for the good - most of us know what it feels like to be compelled into choices that we haven't given birth to, and that generally they are superficial and usually don't "stick". Slowing down the pace of change is often good in that it allows a more organic adaptation and considered reprioritising. While the rapid shifts connected to crisis are often unavoidable, if that's all we have then structurally we end up with a big pile of rubble rather than the lovely extension/expansion we were hoping for.

It's hardly surprising that spirals feature so significantly within sacred symbology - as a representation of what it feels like to journey inward or outward, in ascent or descent, the spiral reflects that it often seems as though history is repeating itself whilst in reality we are moving closer to the goal (even if it's not necessarily the one we initially intended!). Whether we use the spatial metaphor of a descent in search of depth or an ascent to gain awakening, we can often feel caught up in a psychological Groundhog Day as we revisit the same issues within ourselves and the same dynamics within the same relationships.

Sometimes it may feel as though we are making little if any progress, and the lure of the shiny and new can feel like an essential life upgrade that it's hard to say no to. Learning anything via repetition; dance, martial arts or playing a musical instrument, can feel like hard work as we develop muscle memory or lay down those neural pathways.

In working within the wheel of the year, be it in a Heathen, Druid or other setting, we experience in this turning a sense of this repetition at a macrocosmic level. What seems critical in the midst of these big cycles is the degree of awareness that we bring in noticing the often subtle shifts and differences over time and location. Even if we were to celebrate each festival in exactly the same location, the variance in conditions and our own place in the life cycle bring newness with it.

In working in our Zen-Hearth, part of the rationale for integrating Pagan and mindfulness-based approaches is to try and wake-up to the subtleties of this spiralling process. Often we can be in danger of over-codifying our seasonal rituals and swamping ourselves with pre-existing scripts about how things should be. By paying attention to the process of interaction between self and context, we are seeking a type of deep listening to the relevant Genius Loci or Spirit of Place (see the excellent *Wanton Green* for more on this).

Can't see the wood for the trees?

The Western Magical tradition often deals with the rather bizarre paradox of minimising difference and local context ("no really Odin and Mercury are virtually the same - look where they are on the Qabalah!") while at the same time injecting things with sanity challenging hidden meaning (Kenneth Grant's use of gematria being a case in point). Often we can't see the wood for the trees! It might be that we need to opt for some cognitive self-limitation, a type of voluntary simplicity in which we seek a mindful sensitivity to the nuances of localised animism. In the development of my own practice this feels vital in my own attempt to escape the excesses of occult consumerism and neophilia.

While the hardcore enlightenment project of Theravada Buddhism maybe appealing in its thorough engagement with the internal processes of the bodymind, I'm personally more intrigued by the messier adventures of the Buddha's teaching as it encountered the shamanic traditions of cultures it came to. Whether that be the Bon religion, Taoism or Shinto, the interaction between self and context feels vital. In order to escape the traps of either magickal solipsism ("I am a God!") or overly romanticised pantheism, the rediscovery of mindfulness as a dialogue of awakening feels important. As we experience this interplay we can begin to realise that for our insights to continue to be meaningful they have to be expressed via engaged activity. Perhaps this slow, open receptivity to context and place within the cycle of change will allow expressions of "right effort" and "right livelihood" to be more skilful and sustainable.

SD

Deep Chaos: Part Deux

"Man's last and highest parting occurs when, for God's sake, he takes leave of God." Meister Eckhart

Magic can be a funny old business. I recently had an interesting car journey with a friend who had tried to read some of the posts on this blog, and was frankly struggling with the idea that I actually believed that Magic worked.

As a reasoned apologist, I started by stating that I thought that the psychodrama of ritual practice was primarily focused on transforming ourselves. Whatever else Magic may or may not accomplish it aims to transform our own awareness so that we become more effective. By self-willed memetic infection, the change that we seek becomes more likely as we sensitize our perception to themes and opportunities. So far so good, but after this in all honesty my explanations started to get a bit blurry. As I sought to wax lyrical about probability enhancement, chaos theory and the power of placebo, I felt increasingly like some sort of new age snake oil salesman. While these hip sound bites were pointing towards complex and subtle realities, I felt that I was doing a rather shit job at describing why I pursue the spiritual path that I do.

If for a moment I surrender my self-identification as a magical practitioner and ask "what do I actually find myself doing?" the answer is arguably far more interesting and multi-faceted. Stepping back from some sort of spiky, black-clad magical stereotype, the actual phenomena of my spiritual practice is often far from sorcerous go-getting. Looking back through old magical diaries I see lots of hatha yoga, lots of mindfulness practice, mantra work, crazed speculations and wondering. What I tend to see is an exploration of the bodymind and a testing/re-testing of various hypothesis about what might be going on. So think less black-clad Crowley wannabe, more dishevelled Colombo wondering and wandering.

When I first got turned onto the esoteric via the work of Carl Jung, it was his interest in the unconscious and synchronicity that flicked a light switch for me. As my friend and Jung scholar Lloyd Keane might observe, old Carl Gustav was in pursuit of mystery and depth. In reflecting upon my ongoing pursuit of Magic as a spiritual path, it is not an end in itself but rather a set of approaches that make the exploration of Mystery possible. While the passivity of faith sought to continually reassure, Magic often aims to provide a Gnostic toolkit via which the brave (or foolhardy!) may plumb the depths of initiatory possibility.

The fantastic quote from Meister Eckhart highlights that the more we work with something, the more it seems that we need to be willing to let go of how we initially understood it. When we place ourselves on an initiatory journey that seeks to explore the unknown, the spiritual detective must be willing to re-evaluate cherished past orthodoxies that no longer hold as true. This is a high-stakes game in which previous colleagues turn away and in which terms like "heretic" are bandied about. This process of redefinition and conscious surrender is often the work of deep chaos.

Whether we frame such voyages as "crossing the Abyss" or as confronting Apophis, the core process seems similar. We come to a point where language and concepts falter as the Void calls out to our inner ache for liberty. When we push out into the deep waters, what we thought of as "Self" is swallowed up by Leviathan. We are gone, floating in a pregnant darkness where time and direction mean little. Traditions may vary in describing this as an annihilation of Self or in a greater unfolding beyond the egoic, but these are often limited spatial metaphors that we employ in trying to map the numinous.

However these states are induced - be it through sitting meditation, trance dancing, or their spontaneous arising, their impermanence means that eventually a more active expression of consciousness will re-emerge. When we emerge from these states of absorption, while the demands and pleasures of our waking life remain, we cannot return unchanged. Our understanding and the favoured techniques that got us started on the path may no longer feel relevant - and may in fact run contra to new insights gained.

Magic, like anything subtle, is by its very nature difficult to articulate and needs to be subject to on-going revision. Magic for me is strongly related to Heidegger's idea of mood, and it's hard to articulate the power of its performativity as a distant observer. Ariel Glucklich is helpful in trying to capture the idea of "magical consciousness" in his study of magical practitioners in Banaras. For him magic is both relational (between practitioner and client) and it takes place in a liminal state of consciousness in which the micro-analysis of linear causation is suspended. To try to understand Magic outside such an enlivened discourse seems inevitably limited.

Magic by its very nature needs to be immersive and to understand it you need to risk doing it, and in doing it you need to be willing to abandon what you thought it was.

SD

Magick Works?

'Does magick work?' asked a member of the audience at a lecture I gave at a recent Swansea Pagan Moot. Since I once wrote a book called *Magick Works* the simple answer would seem to me to be 'yes', but let's unpack that a little more.

The first issue is whether we can talk about magick working in the same falsifiable, empirically testable sense as a mechanistic science experiment. My answer to this is 'possibly'. I have the privilege of knowing three people who have doctorates in parapsychology in the British Isles. Of these three learned persons (who have not only a great knowledge of psychic stuff but are mean statisticians), one thinks that psychic powers (magick) are bunkum, one thinks there is a real phenomenon at work, and one remains uncertain.

Outside the world of random number generators and Zener cards the scientific analysis of parapsychological phenomena is at least as complex as the science of any social process. But there are methods for dealing with this kind of fuzzy data. Techniques such as phenomenological analysis of texts (such as counting word frequency across a series of accounts) allow us to peer into the quantitative aspects of the human experience. But there are still problems in trying to falsify the claims of the individual magician.

If I cast a spell to get a better job and I'm successful, it's impossible to re-run the experiment of my life without the ritual and see what happens. We do have evidence, across many individuals, that psychological techniques (such as positive thinking, a modern re-statement of magickal practice) do have overall beneficial effects in areas such as being successful at job interviews. But for an individual case, although I may think it was the sigil I built that helped me, it may well be simply that the interviewer really liked my tie and that was the deciding factor that got me the job. Of course given a magical worldview this would still count as a success, since I picked that particular tie that day and that particular interviewer was swayed by my sartorial style.

Then there is the issue that magick isn't really about a simple causal chain; ritual A creates result B. It is, for me, a much more complex process. Being a magician is about being sensitive to, and weaving the web of Wyrd to generate a universe of pleasure, freedom and power (ideally, for all sentient beings). In this sense every act, like Crowley says, is an act of magick.

A while ago I was playing host to two friends from Cornwall. One of them was looking to move into new accommodation and she was trying to get together the deposit required. I'd just been given a gift of £100 and at that moment had a strong sense that I should give this money to her. This thought was encouraged because I'd just read *Psychomagic* by Alejandro Jodorowsky, which talks about the importance (specifically in the context of healing) of symbolic, intuitive magical acts.

Several months later I had the honour of attending an all-night ceremony with three Huichol Indians in the space that my friend was now guardian of. This ceremony, which was an extraordinary event and very powerful for me on many levels, might not have happened were it not for that gift of money many weeks before.

This leads me to another important point. The example given above shows how, from my perspective the 'act of magick' (gifting some money) helped create a reality for me of pleasure, freedom and power. However I would avoid drawing a simple causal chain of events that suggested that I was solely responsible for manifesting that ceremony, months later.

There were many other acts, many actions, many actors in the web of Wyrd between my gift and that event.

Many stories, not least that of King Canute, serve to remind us that, no matter who we think we are, reality is far from under our control. The magician does not in fact stand outside of the universe ordering it about. We may act on the system but we are also acted upon by it, and indeed arise through it. For this reason a wise magician cultivates a good sense of humour; the best defence against hubris, superstition and egomania.

Finally, in answering the question 'does magick work?' we should consider the importance of the imagination. Magical techniques are based on a direct engagement with the imaginative faculty, and it is the imagination that underlies all our culture, art, science and technology. Take the telephone; this technology allows us real-time communication, from mind to mind, across the globe. But this function, this concept, evolved from a dance between the human imagination and direct personal experience of the world (experiment, or as I like to call it the 'gnostic project'). Without the imagination of what might be possible, of building 'what ifs' and 'as ifs' in our minds, we would be incapable of coming up with the applications of our discoveries. This reminds me of Phil Hine's lovely definition; "Magic is a set of techniques and approaches which can be used to extend the limits of achievable reality". Through engaging the imagination, using magical methods, possibilities open up in whatever field of action concerns us. And those possibilities, like the imagination, are endless.

Magick is an exploration of the Mystery, and that Mystery is always receding, like a rainbow, towards the horizon of what we know.

JV

Reyn Til Runa!

Silence in the North

Christmas/Solstice can be a funny time of year - and by "funny" I mean potentially a bit shit. Expectations of spending and busyness often feel at odds with what the rest of the nearby natural world (in the northern latitudes) is doing in terms of retreat, hibernation and the conservation of resources.

In reflecting upon our recent work with "black" magick within our Chaos coven, many of us were aware of the organic flow of the work that people brought to our gathering. Much of the ritual work and spiritual practice reflected a deep need to quieten things down, to release things into the earth so that a process of death, decay and rebirth might begin. Julian writes (in *Magick Works?* - above) about the ways in which our magick might work its wyrd in our lives, and personally I feel that those practices have deepened a process that is inevitably connected to the time of year and place within which I live.

The standstill of the solstice

Whether this internal sense of needing to withdraw is due to lowered serotonin production or just a cyclic response to the exertions of the year, I definitely feel more aware of the more primal aspects of my life - in contrast to the solar surging of the summer months, the need to eat, conserve energy and seek the warmth of shelter feel all the more pronounced. While the spring, summer and autumn were filled with gigs, writing and new projects, I now want to hunker down so as to rest, to heal and prepare for what may be.

As I'm drawn towards the quiet dark my own desire to verbalise and explain seems to fall away - perhaps this is why so many family Christmases are a bit fraught! My own spiritual work has also taken on a more relaxed feel - more time spent on my Zen cushion, or doing gentle bodywork rather than sorcerous doings, or the pursuit of divinatory gnosis. If a dialectic exists between "doing" on one pole and "being" on the other, I'm at the being end, bidding my time for Imbolc, green magick and the beginnings of synthesis.

Within the Chaos Craft schema, winter solstice corresponds to Octarine magick and a sense of the trans-personal. Whether via Mithras, Mabon or the birth of the Christ child, Octarine seems to hold within it death, rebirth and critically the brief pause between the two. Like the top of the in-breath during pranayama, there is potentially much to gain in noticing the space between things where words and deeds hold less sway. However we choose to conceptualise the transpersonal realm, we often experience the limitations of language and the value of acknowledging mystery - may the gods spare us the fragile safety of certainty!

So here's to the Great Spirit, the Mystery and the Turning of the Year! May the forthcoming year be one of Peace, Freedom and Happiness for all of us!

SD

The Way of the Fakir

"When I was 17, I had fasted, I had not slept for 24 hours, and I put staples in a wall to pull ropes through in the outline of my body... I started lashing myself to the wall, legs and torso tight... I wanted an experience right on the edge of death... I had a conscious out-of-body experience... You have a body but it's fluid." Extract from the RE/search interview with Fakir Musafar in *Modern Primitives*.

Having spent a fair amount of time musing over the significance that the Gurdjieff work might have for the contemporary magician, I thought I'd take a bit more time unpacking each of the paths that combine to make up the Fourth Way. If awakening within the Fourth Way entails the activation of the body, heart and mind within "the usual conditions of life", in my mind it's essential that we look at what working with these aspects of Self might look like. At the outset, I'd also add that while using Gurdjieff's language, I don't feel that artificially distinguishing between body, emotions and mind fits well with most of our experiences of reality.

Gurdjieff describes the way of the body as being that of the "Fakir". Perhaps not a term that familiar to the average Westerner, but given his extensive travels throughout the Middle-East (see *Meeting with Remarkable Men*), one that was very familiar to Gurdjieff. The Fakir was generally a contortionist who through training, dedication and a fair degree of masochism, performed amazing feats with their bodies. The way of the Fakir is one in which the starting point of one's journey is the physical body and the use of austerity and asceticism in order to harness its potential. For Gurdjieff the Fakir learns from observation - like a hatha yoga class or five rhythm's dance workshop, we learn best by seeing others seeking enlightenment through the body.

The story of how we relate to our physical selves seems critical to our age. Much ink could be spilt on the way in which the Judeo-Christian and Descartean traditions have led to many of us in the west having an experience of being cut-off or ostracised from our bodies. We can feel like ghosts in the machine - disembodied drivers of unruly vehicles that struggle to stay on the road. So many of us want more, and as we struggle with the sense of psychic fracture, we turn to the body as a possible route for a more visceral, earthy connection.

Magickal modifications

This need to connect has birthed a multiplicity of approaches and responses: martial arts, a multitude of bodywork therapies, tattooing and body modification, being just a few examples of how we are seeking to recapture our journeys by marking them on our bodies. This impulse drove the 17-year-old Roland Loomis to become Fakir Musafar, the father of modern primitivism. Shamanic lore is rich with examples of technologies that use the body as a means of seeking gnosis. Whether via application of weights and constriction, or through consciously seeking bee stings, these animist psychonauts sought a multiplicity of means for inducing consciousness change via the body. I would argue that the stereotype of the pierced chaos mage is as much about this need as it is our love of cyber-punk aesthetics!

This re-visioning of the body as a means of enlightenment fits well with the tantric axiom of "Samsara as Nirvana" i.e. the realm that others see as illusion or impediment is actually the avenue via which the 'higher' centres of emotion and cognition are accessed. To my mind the tantric endeavour is primarily concerned with using the senses and the body as a means of awakening. The primary technologies of mantra, yantra, mudra and nyasa challenge us to find God in the body. These technologies are techniques of extending and intensification - we more fully access the natural by applying 'non-natural' or ultra-natural means.

Make mention of tantra to most people and it conjures images of endless orgies and Sting's long-suffering wife. Whatever the value to be found in neo-tantric practice as a contemporary sex therapy, unless these techniques challenge our conditioning and loosen the blocks to liberation, they are apt to become little more than another hobby (albeit a highly pleasurable one!). Why limit bodily ecstasy to the genitals? The technologies of occult tantra challenge us to open every pore as Shiva/Shakti in union - each moment then becoming a means for accessing Freud's polymorphous perversity.

The Gurdjieff Work's means for engaging with the body similarly challenge the participant to work with the natural in a 'non-natural' manner. The "Movements" are a series of gestures which when put together become dances that pretty much stand alone in captivating the viewer with their mesmerising strangeness. If the goal of the Work is to awaken from a machine-like sleep state, the movements are designed to force the body out of slumber via their running contra to 'natural' tendencies. While an attempt to awaken via the body alone may have limited results in Gurdjieff's schema, if we integrate it with both the heart and mind, it can become the work of the cunning man.

To pursue the work of the magician via ritual and the use of ecstatic technologies means to be in the body. Whether via dance, yoga or sacred sexuality practices, as we bring greater consciousness to bear on the kinaesthetic, so the body transitions and mutates to become expansive and mysterious. Whether via kundalini awakenings or Holy Ghost shaking, the hidden potentialities of the body loosen the armour of our outdated personas, so that we might risk the new vistas of our future Selves.

SD

Green
The Goddess in Green

Bright sunshine strikes the ground. The air remains cold but, in defiance of the low temperatures, impetuous bulbs thrust their shoots skyward. The year stirs and, as the light is turned up, the first insects wake. As I clean our country temple (last used some three years ago) sleepy ladybirds shuffle around the window frames. An usher moth, disturbed from the woodpile, flutters into the brilliant air.

It is our Imbolc ceremony, time of purification, of Green magick and of love.

There are snowdrops on the altar and bright bronze vessels, polished and gleaming.

It's that Lupercalia moment

We begin our work with a ritual led by our Wiccan Sister. The men are asked to leave the temple (we stand outside, hopping around in the chilly afternoon to keep warm). Inside the women invoke:

"THIS IS THE FEAST OF THE DAWN OF THE YEAR WHERE WE SEEK TO RENEW OURSELVES. TO REINVENT OURSELVES. TO PURIFY OUR OUTER AND INNER LIVES IN THE NAME OF THE WHITE GODDESS, MISTRESS OF THE SACRED FLAME. FOR THIS IS THE MYSTERY: THE GODDESS RENEWS HERSELF AFTER THE BIRTH OF THE SOLSTICE SUN, EVEN AS HER BLOOD RENEWS HER MAGIC EACH MONTH SO THE EVER FLOWING CYCLES OF LIFE, DEATH AND RESURRECTION ARE MAINTAINED BY HER TRANSFORMATIONS!"

The Guardian Priestess holds a sword to the breast of each man at the temple door:

THOSE WHO ARE PREPARED TO BE PURIFIED MAY ENTER THE TEMPLE. Each participant is asked individually "WHAT DO YOU SEEK?" They may answer "I SEEK PURIFICATION/REDEDICATION/CONSECRATION".

Directed to enter the temple and kneel at the altar, one of the She-Wolf Priestesses will scourge the participant 21 times, while another reads in their ear:

"WE ARE DAUGHTERS OF THE SEASON AND WE KNOW THAT THE COLD OF WINTER PURIFIES ALL, AS THE ICE PURIFIES THE WATERS AND THE FROSTS PURIFY THE EARTH, SO THE HEAT OF THE FIRE PURIFIES OUR BODIES AND THE SCOURGE PURIFIES OUR SOULS. WE ARE REMADE IN THE FORGES OF THE TRIPLE GODDESS OF INSPIRATION AND MAGIC, SHE WHO BRINGS RENEWAL AND INSPIRATION."

Participant repeats after the Priestess:

"WITH THE RENEWAL OF THE YEAR I WILL RE-DEDICATE MYSELF TO MAGIC BY THE PURITY OF MY WILL."

The women then make their own purifications. They in turn kneel and are scourged by the men.

The temple thus opened, it's time for the 'Oxytocin Breast Love-In'. The aim of this ritual is to address the issue of breast cancer in women (and is offered as a healing rite for one individual in particular). No-one is certain of the endogenous mechanism which means that the more children a woman has the less her chance of developing breast cancer. However one suggestion is that the protective effect derives from the oxytocin generated by the embraces of mother and child. Our statement of intent is "We would love to hear of many more breast cancers made well'. In this ritual we first dip into the oxytocin deliciousness, laying down in the warm temple and sucking our thumbs, cuddled together. From here we go out into the cold evening air. Down into the garden where snowdrops peep above the leaf litter. Walking around a tree we summon the other side of oxytocin, the defensive aspect of this hormone that strengthens boundaries of the group against outsiders (and defends the healthy self from illness). We follow a green path (actually a long garden hose) I have arranged that snakes past the garden pond and runs through a gateway (made of decorative ironwork wrought into the shape of many hearts). Once each person has passed the gate, releasing the power they have summoned into the Noosphere, we stand together and watch the waxing moon.

Back into the temple the next ritual is a Spring Cleaning. This practice involves meditating on the sound of ocean waves, letting the waters wash over us, cleaning and scouring us pure. Then the soundscape changes to that of songbirds in a verdant woodland. We meditate on the building up of the spring. The growing of the light, the land and ourselves. A simple but powerful practice.

A ritual in praise of the Goddess Green Tara is next. We worship her to inspire in us every sort of perfection. We chant her mantra as we inflame ourselves with alcohol and hot chilli peppers. This is a devotional rite until the moment when we occupy the perspective of the Goddess herself. Looking back through her eyes at our own bodies, willing us towards perfection. Then, as one, we snap back from this combined awareness and into our bodies. Inflamed and inspired. We banish this puja with Coprolalia.

Our next practice is the alethiometer, a divination system presented by our Brother featuring Rory's Story Cubes. This oracle provides a fresh method of divination composed of simple images that, unlike the tarot or runes, doesn't come creaking under the weight of generations of symbolic associations.

A medicine ritual is next, with songs and acoustic music, while we open our hearts using a snuff of sacred tobacco as our ally.

Then it's time to perform the Mass of Green Baphomet. This rite is to charge a jar of incense that is part of a longer working by a Sister who is involved in psychogeographic magick. The barbarous invocation of Baphomet has been 'greened' by adding the bīja 'Om' to the text and by being sung in the style of a Sanskrit mantra. My Sister and I feel the force grow, rising like new sap through us. The energy of Green Baphomet seeps into the scented resins we hold between us. Gradually it fades to a still steady glow; the jar pulses with power.

In preparation for the end of the workings our Sister who opened the temple now calls upon the triple Bride. Each participant lights a green candle and these are placed in a large mixing bowl full of earth in the centre of the circle.

Fire & Light

"BRIGANTIA, BRIGHIDE, BRIDGET, BRIDE! O LADY OF THE TRIPLE MAGICS, PURIFY US WITH THE ICE FIRE OF THE SEASON AS THE FROST PURIFIES THE EARTH, AND THE SCOURGE PURIFIES THE SOUL, AND IN SO DOING REKINDLE THE FIRE WITHIN US FOR YOUR MAGIC IS THE MYSTERY OF RENEWAL!

I CALL TO BRIDE, TO THE FLAME OF CREATIVITY, FOR THE BARD TRANSFORMS WORDS TO SONG AND IN INSPIRATION REVITALISES OUR SOULS

I CALL TO BRIDE, TO THE FIRE OF HEALING WHICH TRANSFORMS OUR BODIES FROM IMBALANCE TO EASE, AND IN BRINGING US WELL BEING REINVIGORATES OUR SOULS

I CALL TO BRIDE, TO THE POWER OF THE SMITH WHO REFINES ORE TO PURE METAL AND IN TEACHING US CREATION REJUVENATES OUR SOULS.

O PERFECT PEACE PROFOUND OF UTMOST UNEXISTENCE INFINITE, ETERNAL, NIL, UNBORN, UNBEING, UNBOUNDED UNILLUMINATE, UNMANIFEST, THOU ART. FROM THOU WE ORIGINATE OURSELVES: UTTER FORTH THE WILL WORD: LIGHT!"

"LIGHT!" (Everyone)

The bowl of candles is still burning for our final ceremony, part of our ongoing political magickal process. Of this matter I must keep silent except to say that an icon of the rite is the flower reproduced below:

Sitting outside that night, though the air is cold, I feel strangely warm. Care is here amongst my Brothers & Sisters, and love, and a sense of clear direction. There is movement, intention and brave renewal, spring has sprung and magick is abroad.

JV

Children in the Circle –
Paganism, Spirituality and our Families

Hanging up decorations to celebrate Yule, carving pumpkins at Halloween, dancing the Maypole and more - all of these are at once modern Pagan activities, folk customs, and stuff that kids can get involved with. Those of us who have the honour and delight to be parents get to engage in some very interesting questions when it comes to the relationship between our own spiritual practices and our kids. So what is the context for what's going on? In a significantly secular culture such as Britain (around 25% of English citizens describe their religion as 'none') there is a tendency to think that spirituality (or the apparent lack of it) is down to personal choice and conscience. Britain is also a spiritually diverse landscape, and the arguable origin of a number of new religious paths. It's also true that the social function of religion in Britain is perhaps different from that of the USA. So with these considerations in mind how do we, as families, integrate our own spirituality with raising children?

Hanging up the Yule/Christmas/Mithrasmas/Winterval decorations is a good example. This is an embodied practice, one that we can give multiple meanings to. A ritual like this can be something children enjoy and participate in. In my household I describe what we're doing in, what I hope, is a very open-ended way: 'We're making the house look fun because it's dark and we're going to have a few days holiday where we can watch movies, eat nice food, and snuggle by the open fire. We are celebrating the fact of the longest night, the beginning of the New Year, and the slow return of the light'. Unless they go all Jehovah's Witness when they get older, my approach is also I hope, broad enough that they can appreciate what we did in Pagan, Humanist, Atheist, Christian or other terms and not find it problematic. Also, they don't have to join in. I'm totally happy to put the tree up and install the ivy myself, but naturally they want to help.

Of course there are lots of parts of my own spiritual life from which my children are excluded. All of the esoteric groups I work with maintain policies that preclude the admission of anyone under the age of at least 18 (even in the informal world of Wicca 30 years ago it was really difficult for me to get involved in a group when I was 16). However in other cultures these things differ. Children are most certainly present at ceremonies such as the Healing Dance of the San people from South Africa. In this rite dancing and singing continues long into the night as people are possessed by spirits (an event, which in that culture is often attended by bleeding through the nose). Mothers sit on the sand with their babies and, at least before they get tired and bored, the younger San kids run around the outside of the ritual space, pretending to get possessed and generally taking the piss out of the shamans in the circle. Just as one might expect.

One of the benefits of my own Pagan spirituality is that it allows me to include my children in the public and gentle ceremonies of celebration (such as the ones that take place at St Nectan's Glen, and at many other sacred sites in the British Isles), as well as a selection of domestic traditions. Because these traditions are rooted in the flow of the seasons they are open to interpretation and elaboration in many different ways. Intelligent children (and of course my kids are really bright) readily understand this. My eldest son, many years ago, pointed out that the sun coming back from the solstice of Yule was the same as Aslan in *The Lion the Witch and the Wardrobe.* And that this was basically the same as the story of Osiris and also Jesus. Personally I tend to avoid names of deities (though we all have a soft spot for Ganesh and through the medium of Marvel comics both my kids are getting more interested in Norse mythology) and instead talk about what we're doing as people connected to the landscape we're in. It's all about relationships and perspectives. So at the Equinox I explain that this time is about noticing that light and dark are equal, and realising that this is one of only two days in the year where the day and night length is pretty much equal all across the whole world. No deities, no rules, no dogma, just a scientific fact that we're choosing to notice and celebrate.

nomnomnom

As well as including our children in accessible and culturally appropriate aspects of our spirituality we can also learn from them. For Lammas this year, at the suggestion of my eldest son, we made special biscuits to celebrate the fact that the harvest had come. This has become something of a theme (I mean home-made biscuits! What's not to like?). And so for this Equinox my children made two batches of biscuits that we shared with participants at a public Pagan ritual we attended. Chocolate ones for the dark of the year, and banana and vanilla ones for the light.

Thus, my kids have built for themselves a family and community tradition. I only hope that they don't follow through on some of the more grotesque suggestions they seem to be considering for their Halloween recipe!

JV

Changing Perspectives

I was recently on top of a hill, sitting within a ring of low trees and gorse bushes. The sky overhead, a classic spring fractured scene of white clouds, bright blue and sweeping skeins of rain. I'd chosen to invoke an ally, a particular spirit to help in a little practice that I call 'changing perspectives'.

The process is simple, something I learnt spontaneously as a child. One begins by lying down, focusing on the breath and getting comfortable. On a warm day one might sink into a little sleep and that's fine. The trick is, on waking to keep the gaze low. Open the eyes, roll onto your belly and look at the earth.

Titanic structures in miniature

There they are, all the little creeping things, the growers, the flourishers, tiny lives which, looked at the right way, take place around huge citadels. In this case the 'huge citadels' are bracken fronds. They are around twelve inches long, tipped

Chaos Craft

with unfurling, fractal heads, spirals curled up against spirals, curled up against spirals... They are huge, at least for the tiny lives that pass below. What is the smallest one I can see with the naked eye? I watch a translucent aphid pace the great length of a grass stem.

Letting my gaze rise a little I can see the bracken stems, marching out across the grey-brown matting of last year's growth that carpets the ground. Between these proud green towers creatures hum, and buzz and flutter. The bright sun catches their wings and they shine. Fat raindrops, left by one of the recent showers, glint like futurist windows on stalks and leaves.

Now looking higher, towards the gigantic towering trees and birds, great flapping dinosaurs intent on devastating the insect nation. And higher still until my eyes are following the patterns at the leading edge of clouds, and a tiny black mote which is a hawk soaring. I watch it circling upwards until it is lost into the phosphenes of my vision as the bright sun erupts from behind a cloud.

The sun dazzles with its brightness. I bring to mind the fact that I'm on a planet, resting on the side of the earth currently pointing towards a star. And that star is one of countless billons in our galaxy.

Then I open my attention as wide as I can, try to take in everything, to know and feel that I live in a universe whose centre is everywhere and circumference nowhere found. And that the 'I' who I am can travel through these perspectival changes, and is ceaselessly arising as the awareness of all things, from the subatomic to the galactic.

Letting go of these imaginings and settling back to baseline. Allowing the cognitive flexibility created by the practice to gently fade into the ongoing flow of awareness. Breathe, smile.

To conclude this practice 1 normally recommend some light food and tea.

JV

On Compassion, Community and Conflict

One of the three treasures of Buddhism is the Sangha. This is the community of practice. Those people around us who support us in what, in Western magick, we might call The Great Work or perhaps the process of Illumination. As someone who thrives on close collaboration (the majority of the books on which my name appears are co-authored texts) and communal activity (since the age of fifteen much of my esoteric work has happened in groups) the Sanhga is essential to me. Of course it's not like that for everyone; some folks really thrive on working alone, or perhaps with just one other person. More accurately, most of us (even gregarious me) will have periods in which we need solitary practice, and other times when we want to come together with others.

I've been fortunate to work within many organisations over the years; ranging from The Order of Bards, Ovates and Druids, Wiccan covens, native shamanic settings, The Arcane Magical Order of the Knights of Shambhala (AMOOKOS) and, for the last ten years (though not to the exclusion of those other groups) with The Illuminates of Thanateros. While the style and focus (though perhaps not the ultimate project) of these groups is pretty diverse, there is a shared commonality of function in that they are all designed to support and nurture the people within them. And as part of this support there also has to be a compassionately critical process at work too; where we help each other to unpick our difficulties and to transcend our own (often self-created) problems.

All these groups necessarily share culture; signs, stories and in-jokes. This is part of what makes a community. There is the need not only to build up the group mind or egregore, but also to figure out how people are admitted to and indeed excluded from the group.

A wrathful deity this morning...

Policing of the boundary of a group is something that different communities deal with in different ways. What becomes apparent to anyone who spends time in any human society (esoteric or otherwise) is that exclusion is often a painful process. Human beings are (mostly) highly socialised creatures so kicking someone out of a group isn't usually an easy thing. But in these situations, remembering a few Buddhist insights can be helpful. Even if those people we exclude have done harm to our community, or indeed are likely to still cause trouble when removed from our immediate orbit, it is compassion that we should deploy when presented with these situations.

'Compassion is the vice of kings...', writes Crowley in his Book of the Law. One interpretation of this is that 'kings' (i.e. people engaged with the discovery and pursuit of their True Will, the heroes or vira of tantrism) can afford to have genuine compassion. When we take a decision, even a hard and difficult one, a king will do so in a way that is free from vindictive malice and is instead predicted on a desire to see all parties liberated (or illuminated or whatever).

Compassion is something that, possibly more than any other behaviour in my view, marks out the successful and engaged magician. Not some wishy-washy sympathy for others but a genuine lived concern for the well-being of those around us, even, and sometimes especially, for those difficult people. One of the top techniques I know for this is the practice of Tonglen (essentially absorbing the suffering in the world around us and transforming it into compassion and liberation). Cultivating compassion plugs us into bodhichitta, explained nicely in Sam Webster's book *Tantric Thelema*, empowering our magick in part by making us viscerally cognisant of the Hermetic view that all things are, in essence, one. A lack of compassionate capacity, and the subsequent sense of the world as full of 'the (evil) Other', as well as that hoary old chestnut 'lust of result' goes a long way to explaining why angry and malicious people are rubbish at magick, spending their time flinging curses at the world that simply don't work.

The esoteric traditions of the Himalayas are pretty hardcore when it comes to expressing compassion (showing us that being compassionate certainly doesn't look like being an interpersonal doormat!). There are all kinds of fearsome forms of the Buddha that are about destroying the obstacles which stand between us and Enlightenment, and acting swiftly to liberate us from suffering. This liberation can be a hard and painful process. If we are ill we may need the poison drained from us and that's best done fast, fully and with care. The insight of Buddhism (the drive towards compassion), is balanced with what one might describe as a Tantric view; that we should aim to accept the world as it is, recognising the divine in all things, without falling into aversion. The poison may need to come out - but both it, and the pain that attends its removal; this is also part of the sacred totality.

The blending of these elements is especially important in group settings. We aim to interact with each other in a compassionate way, and also we realise that the world is as it is, and even in those things we find difficult we should aim to find the sacred, and through those things opportunities for Illumination. These two pillars of practice mean that as we enter challenging situations our compassion is fed by our recognition of the sacred moment of the Now just as it is (warts and all).

Down to earth spirituality

This recognition, of the presence of the sacred in every moment, allows compassion to arise even for those people whom we find difficult. It allows us to act (albeit sometimes to painfully prick the poison boil) without feelings of hatred or the need to take refuge in a (suffering-tastic) de-humanising attitude. Our orientation to events changes, so while we may still feel that something is a bad situation we don't so much rise above it but engage with it in a way that betokens a caring motivation, a stance that nourishes rather than depletes our psychic reserves. This allows groups to flourish and develop a culture of mutual respect and empowerment (both internally and in their relations with others). It also helps them successfully adapt to inclusion and exclusions, to develop what has been called 'collective wisdom', which in magic-speak is the empowerment of the community's egregore.

In the face of the slings and arrows of fortune, and the vicissitudes of human nature, working magick in communities can be a huge challenge (as well as being, for folks like me, greatly rewarding). So let us have compassion for ourselves too, and practice the wry grin of the bodhisattva. After all nobody said The Great Work, or indeed our refuge in the Sangha, was going to be easy!

JV

Me and my Monkish Ways

In the rich and varied path that I have travelled as an erstwhile spiritual adventurer, there was a period when I longed to don the brown robe of St. Francis in order to become a monk. When I talk to friends about this desire, those who know me well are rarely surprised. They seem to see in me certain traits or passions that are still present even after being with my partner for over 20 years and having two children.

So I've got to wondering what they see in me and how this might fit with Gurdjieff's depiction of the way of the monk. In the Fourth Way schema the Monk is viewed as being the path of the second "room" or centre and as being connected to the heart and the emotions. In this realm, the aspirant channels the multiplicity of emotions towards the greater goal of devotion or bhakti. For me this made a lot of sense; the identity turmoil that I experienced in my early teens to mid-twenties was largely contained by a devotional fervour that I directed towards Jesus and the Saints.

I still feel that the path of the heart is vital. While it can risk sentimental naivety, and the maintenance of the "believer" in the position of Child, to ignore its call is hazardous. Large parts of the Western Buddhist and Magickal communities are at risk of becoming overly intellectual in their bookish pursuit of wisdom. Perhaps we have confused true gnosis with simply knowing about stuff.

Now it's not all doom and gloom! The collective unconscious is a beautiful thing. Whether via the discovery of more devotional meditative traditions (e.g. Pure Land) or via the excellent work of Scarlet Imprint (see Peter Grey's *The Red Goddess* and the *Devoted* anthology), we can see the development of true heart depth borne from practice.

Devotional practice may take many forms...

For me the path of faith and devotion were ultimately not enough. I needed knowledge and an internal language or yoga so as to journey into inner space. As a Psychonaut needing to explore, I was no longer content with being spoon-fed certainties. To use Scott Peck's trajectory I had to move from childhood, through the rebellion of adolescence and towards the integration of adulthood - but maturity without passion, emotion and longing? No thank you, not for me!

Gurdjieff believed that each person by disposition would tend to gravitate naturally towards one of the three ways of being and the nature of the "Work" was to access those aspects of Self that came less naturally. As we work towards spiritual holism via integrating the insights of body, mind and heart, I think that the nature of love's expression is transformed.

Whether via deepening our grasp of Agape or wrestling with the implications of "love under Will" as we reach towards that more integral position, is it possible for the expression of the heart to become more expansive? In response to this wondering, a beloved magical sister Lilavirinanda 108 has articulated the idea of "Big Love". Borne from a heady fusion of tantric sadhana, chaos praxis and integral insight, Big Love asks us to expand ever outwards; to move beyond love as a limited power exchange between enamoured egos. Love as an expression of devotion to "the other" (whether human lover, friend or deity) doesn't cease, rather via a process of continually folding back it becomes more refined and responsive.

Whatever the focus of our devotion on the vertical axis, whether our passion is for an ideal or a personified archetypal form ("God"), from an integral perspective any claims to spiritual advancement are hollow if they fail to engender great "Metta" or loving-kindness. For our Magick to grow-up, it has to extend to those beings on the horizontal i.e. to other creatures.

During the Magickal revival much has been made of the way in which our forebears used sorcery to "nobble" those in their way. Defensive and indeed aggressive magicks may well have a valid role in a world in which injustices give the oppressed few other means of redress. If however, we fail to evolve beyond "an eye for and eye and a tooth for a tooth" we may all end up blind and eating soup through a straw! Traditional Witches may rightly point out that the Wiccan Rede's "and it harm none, do what thou wilt" is Gardner's own very modern re-working of Crowley, but I still think it points to a way of living that is worth pursuing. So mote it be indeed!

SD

Orange
Nina Simone Alchemical Orange Magick Mashup

Orange begins the data-download of the light half of the year. The weather swings wildly from brilliant sun, through glowering stratus to sparkling showers of rain, a cut-up climate. Eggs appear, laid by both Easter Bunnies and my hens. Orange magick is transmitted by the sephira of Hod, communicated by Thrice Great Hermes.

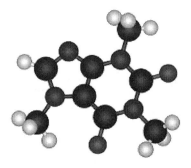

Vivacious veve

Our first work is the 'Voodoo Coffee Morning' a rite of celebration. We praise caffeine, that loquacious molecular messenger, decode its veve (the molecular diagram of $C_8H_{10}N_4O_2$) and sip strong black coffee. Fortified by this stimulating medicine, our next rite is presented by TP808 - the full ritual text of which is given here. Chaos magick, as a style of occultism, is sometimes characterised as being too often about silly rituals that lack depth. However the ritual below, although it uses non-standard esoteric iconography, is far from a superficial, unconsidered working. As well as the ritual itself, TP808 describes the symbolic and metaphysical structures that this rite articulates:

Orange Magick - The Nina Murmuration. 13-04-13

"Music is freedom" - Nina Simone
"We always thought of music as psychic resistance."
Bobby Gillespie.

4 Nina Simone albums in the four quarters.

"This is a good time to introduce you to the heart beat of our organization, the pulse of everything that we do: it centers around the drums and of course if you think about that really seriously you know that your entire life is centered around your heart beat, and that's rhythm is it not?"

Recite Westwind lyrics.

STATEMENT OF INTENT - the aim of this ritual is to time travel using soundwaves. Working with the Deleuzian notion of the "fold":

"The fold is the general topology of thought... 'inside' space is topologically in contact with the 'outside' space... and brings the two into confrontation at the limit of the living present." Deleuze, *Foucault* (University of Minnesota Press, 2000) p. 118-19.

The ritual space is;

"groundless depth from which irrupts something that creates its own space and time. It is not the line that is between two points, but the point that is at the intersection of several lines."

Deleuze, *Pourparlers* (Minuit, 1990) p. 219

[Quotes taken from *GILLES DELEUZE the architecture of space and the fold* by Matthew Krissel].

The ritual also considers Dogen's concept of existence-time (Uji):

"The way the self arrays itself is the form of the entire world. See each thing in this entire world as a moment of time:

"Things do not hinder one another, just as moments do not hinder one another. The way-seeking mind arises in this moment. A way-seeking moment arises in this mind. It is the same with practice and with attaining the way.

Thus the self setting itself out in array sees itself. This is the understanding that the self is time."

See Shobogenzo Chapter 11 discussed by Norman Fischer at the *Buddhist Pagan blog*.

Finally, the ritual also draws upon the concept of quantum foam:

"...a qualitative description of subatomic space time turbulence at extremely small distances... At such small scales of time and space, the Heisenberg uncertainty principle allows energy to briefly decay into particles and antiparticles and then annihilate without violating physical conservation laws. As the scale of time and space being discussed shrinks, the energy of the virtual particles increases. According to Einstein's theory of general relativity, energy curves space-time. This suggests that - at sufficiently small scales - the energy of these fluctuations would be large enough to cause significant departures from the smooth space time seen at larger scales, giving space time a "foamy" character." Wiki. See also MAGIC Telescopes (Major Atmospheric Gamma-ray Imaging Cherenkov Telescopes).

PATHWAY - The ritual uses energy fluctuations generated by drumming and archival recordings of Nina Simone to fold in past and future to this moment now. As a group we drum along with the two pieces of music, the first using our bodies as instruments and the second using noise making machines (drums/rattles.) We become a machinic assemblage; the murmuration is the sound of sound being simultaneous and multiple in the same moment.

> "The beauty of the assemblage is that, since it lacks organization, it can draw into its body any number of disparate elements. The book itself can be an assemblage, but its status as an assemblage does not prevent it from containing assemblages within itself or entering into new assemblages with readers, libraries, bonfires, bookstores, etc."
> Nina Simone - *Nina* (From "*It Is Finished*' 1974)

Body percussion.

#ends

(Improv- glossolalia Nina-nina-nina, murmuration, murmur, murmur murmuration, communication in this place and space Nina-nina-nina Unify us, don't divide us, etc.)

We also draw upon Starhawk's description of immanence as a walk on a beach (in *Dreaming the Dark* Chapter 3 - "Thought-Forms; Magic as Language p-15-16 to "even God...") accompanied by hammered African thumb piano to induce trance. Then expand upon this with a visualization of the same beach at night time, the experience of merging with an orange gelatinous sphere and the visual stimulus of a fire giving off orange embers spiralling into the night sky;

> "And then kerjillions of stars start to shine
> And Icy comets go whizzing by
> And everything's shaking with a strange delight
> And this is it: the enormous night"

Laurie Anderson - *My Eyes - from Strange Angels -* 1989)

Beach visualization orange sphere, bonfire, covered in orange membrane. Sea, stars, warmth.

Westwind blow ye gentle
Over the shores of yesterday
My sun is brown and over
Here within my heart they lay they lay

Westwind with your wisdom
Gather all the young for me
Black cloud hanging over
Nest your bosom strong and free

Got each gallon water is plane
Got each gallon water is plane
Cos I am the soil from which they came
I am the soil from which they came

So Westwind with your splendour
Take my people by the hand
Spread your glory sunshine off
And unify my promised land

Nina Simone, *Westwind* (From 'Black Gold' 1970 written by Miriam Makeba)

The pieces of music are based on African traditional drum patterns and are filtered through Nina Simone's political commitment to civil rights, anti-racism, Black power and the struggle for justice for people of colour and other oppressed groups. An apposite theme on this day when people are processing the death of Margaret Thatcher. As a group we bring Pagan drum patterns to the mix; we are forced to find a space in the music that accommodates our rhythms and also to listen to each other so that we create a horizontal (with each other) and vertical (with the music) matrix of sound that speaks to a) each other now and b) the past, simultaneously in a sound driftwork.

LINK TO SYMBOLIC CARRIER - eating the orange segment to create a virtual and psychick circuit - prior to the start of drumming, the circle is established by the group taking a segment each and placing it into someone else's mouth. We bite into the fruit at the same time synchronising time, place, space and taste buds. The introduction to the ritual echoes the intro speech given by Nina Simone in Windward - echoic time shift. This is only revealed to other participants once they hear the music. Noise making machines also symbolically link all elements of the ritual.

The tantric outer/inner/secret structure of the ritual -

Outer - time travel as explained above

Inner - Strange Angel themes of Robert Mapplethorpe/AIDS/bereavement/Right Wing Censorship of Art/Walter Benjamin's critique of modernity- "History is an angel, being blown backwards into the future. History is a pile of debris and the angel wants to go back and fix things, to repair the things that have been broken but there is a storm blowing from Paradise and the storm keeps blowing the angel backwards into the future, and this storm is called progress...")

Secret - another (unstated) purpose of this ritual is for me to connect with my drum and find out what its relationship to my magick is...

INTENSE GNOSIS - trance brought about through drumming, listening and visualisation.

FIRE - out into the kerjillions of stars spiralling to infinity, devisualisation moving out of liminal space back to the here-now. Back to the beach - the return of the orange membrane to the ground - to be called upon again when needed. Eating a Jaffa cake, drinking orange Tango

FORGET

The Alan Partridge Banishing

AHA!
Rooarrrrrrr!!

TP808

An orange meditation on non-attachment and love comes next. For this each participant takes an orange and mindfully appreciates this fruit (an unscripted similarity with the previous ceremony creating a recursive feedback loop in the ritual arc). The fruit reminds us of the saffron coloured robes of Buddhist monks or the orange garb of the Shivite sadhu, while peeling it we consider non-attachment. We see that we are all flow and that any 'being' is temporary, illusionary. But in understanding non-attachment we do not fall into a solipsistic or disconnected state. Instead with our attachments gone we can peel back apparent reality and enjoy the fruit of experience. More than this we can know love, the bliss of the world and the joy of communion. This comes as we each take a segment and place it on our mouths, biting down together we share the common experience of orange magic, of the bounty and love of the world, of sweetness and nourishment.

Brother Pelagius provides another ritual:

Three Mages Alchemy Rite.

This working was connected to Orange magick via my own relationship with Mercury as the patron of both communication and alchemy. The purpose of the working was to visualise a situation that we wished to transform in our lives and to use the potency of our anxiety/fears about the situation to fuel willed change.

Transmutation from A to Z

The schema used was inspired by the work of Michael Kelly found in his books *Apophis* and *Dragonscales* in which we find the figures of the Black, White and Red mages. For me these correspond to the alchemical stages of nigredo, albedo and rubedo, and our rite sought to use these three states to integrate our unconscious, super-conscious and conscious minds.

After imbibing the dark sacrament of Guinness, we imagined our current situation at night, coated with the fluid tar of our fears. These nightside emissions were not to be rejected, but used to fuel our desires.

Next we opened our eyes to the bright flame of the superconscious. The White Mage greets us and shows us our idealised goal and the changes in ourselves that are necessary in bringing forth such transformations. We cannot dwell here long, for if our work is to become more than a pipedream, it must be born of blood.

So we return to the realm of Midgard and the Red Mage. The flame is now transformed through potent alchemical filters so that the world is seen through a blood soaked hue (okay so we're actually now looking at the candle through bits of red cellophane). The idealised state needs to be earthed in reality as we channel the dark energy of our fears so they can be put to more skilful ends.

Many rituals are for sharing. The non-attachment and love ritual with the oranges I was subsequently able to share at another two meetings. The first of these was at the far end of Cornwall with friends from a South American shamanic path. The third time was at the request of a Priestess (who had been present at the second performance) to share the technique in a circle cast on the north Cornish coast. In that third circle stood a Native American Woman who, later that night, shared song and skill (and delightfully strident opinion) with the company. We traded chants, some from the British Isles, some from the States. I offered a song, which the Grandmother medicine had taught me, sung to the insistent rhythm of the Grandfather medicine's water drum.

That simple rite, as easy as you like, peeling an orange (and I know it's been done before; there is, as they say, nothing new under the sun) has popped up in three circles and crossed the paths of native British, South American and North American cultures. Techniques are shared, the world is enchanted, communication magick unites us.

So (as the caffeine kicks in) what next? Well that orange magick vibe reminds me of cut-ups and the excellent experiments of Thee Temple of Psychick Youth and their descendants. Reading *The Psychick Bible* I'm inspired to revisit some of those methods. Now where did I put my old dream machine?

JV, TP808, SD and members of The Western Watchtower

Bardic Inspiration

I remember the first time I really got turned on to poetry; it was while listening to *Sergeant Pepper's Lonely Hearts Club Band* when I was in my early teens. Here was this fantastic world of opulence and decadence where sitars swirled, acid was dropped and Aleister Crowley stuck out his baldy head amongst the starlets and icons. Those moustachioed boys in their lurid band suits captured the spirit of the age not only via their music but also the lyrical vibrancy contained in tracks like *Lucy in the Sky with Diamonds*, *Within*, *Without You* and *A Day in the Life*. This album had a truly magical impact on me, and shaped the direction of my spiritual journey in ways that few books ever have.

Occultnik hipsters from the previous century

In thinking back to my own beginnings in paganism and magical practice, I was initially drawn to the path of Druidry and the emphasis on poetic inspiration that is found in the role of the Bard. Sadly many early druid revivalists (most probably influenced by Freemasonry) projected a rather linear grade system onto Strabo's observation that there were three groupings or classes within the Celtic priesthood, and had placed the Bard at the bottom of the heap. Thankfully, many contemporary druid Orders (while retaining a three grade system to enable a holism in magical training) are re-emphasising the mythic and historical centrality of the poet as custodian of tradition and inspiration.

Within the Druid tradition the idea of poetic expression is innately linked to the concept of Awen, or Spirit of Inspiration. Mythically speaking, Bardic inspiration and the Awen are inextricably linked to the tale of the great poet Taliesin, who ingests this spirit via a magical elixir. As the brew was intended for dark Cerridwen's son, not the nascent Bard, she pursues him in a fit of pique. With the elixir on board he's not so easy to catch, and so ensues the now legendary shape-shifting showdown as she pursues him across the verdant Welsh landscape.

Regular readers of our blog will be familiar with the way in which we as magicians are seeking to describe the circular relationship that exists between magic and art. Shifts in consciousness can be accessed through art and the creative expression itself can entail the same internal processes as more formal meditative or ritual practices. Whatever the medium employed - be it dance, website design or good cooking - the connection between human creativity and spiritual aspiration feels fundamental. Unfortunately the need to keep reminding myself of this often highlights the sense of disconnect many of us get caught in as we lose sight of the sense of spontaneity and "Flow" that we can experience when we truly immerse ourselves in the act of creation.

The idea of Flow (see the work of Mihaly Csikszentmihalyi) - that sense of relaxed productivity that enables us to express our Self - can extend out to all areas of life where creativity and fluidity are of benefit. For me this idea of Flow also connects to the tantric concept of Sahaja, or naturalness and spontaneity. This idea of seeking to experience ourselves as more fluid and shifting can often help as adapt to our Postmodern world; seeing the self more as a river moving through an ever changing landscape, rather than a pool with fixed parameters.

Now this is all well and good, but how do we access this state of creative flow? Going back to the tale of Taliesin and the druid tradition, I think that there are a couple of pointers that can aid our journey:

The Role of Stillness - Of course I'm going to mention mindfulness practice! Cerridwen employs the young Gwion Bach (who was to become Taliesin) to tend the cauldron containing the elixir for a year and a day. So he sits, and he sits - listening to the wisdom of the old man Morda as they tend the cauldron together.

From the perspective of aiding the flow of the poetic, this represents a profound listening to the self. In contrast to those traditions that promote a distrust of our intuition, the path of Bardic inspiration is one in which the deepest stirrings of our souls need to be attended to, be it Walt Whitman's sense of nature mysticism or Rumi's longing for the beloved. We are more likely to contact the poetic if we are able to access the fires of our passion.

Driven by Darkness - Once He has imbibed the Awen, Taliesin flees the oncoming wrath of Cerridwen. Cerridwen as the dark mother pursues him and doing so forces him to access those shamanic states that make transformation possible. The darker aspects of ourselves are often storehouses of poetic power that we need to access in order grow and develop. Into the Shadow we not only repress those aspects of our lives that we fear, but also the best parts of ourselves that we cannot acknowledge. The glory of Art is that it often provides a conduit via which our darkness can flow without overwhelming us.

Connection to the Elements and the three realms - In a way similar to much tantric technology, the arising of spontaneous, natural flow often comes through an increased awareness of the natural world and the body. Perhaps unsurprisingly then, most contemporary Druid orders include in the foundation of their training a thorough focus on the elements and the three worlds (earth, sky and sea). As Taliesin seeks to escape his pursuer it seems significant that the animals that they shift into embody each of these three realms.

Most of us are acutely aware how barren our lives can feel when we feel the absence of flow and creative juiciness in our lives. To contact our own darkness and connection to the body involves commitment - for Gwion Bach to become Taliesin meant job loss, dealing with confrontation and the transformation of his body. Dangerous I know, but worth the risk. As they say in the British Druid Order - "Be the Awen!"

SD

The Gate of Baphomet

All participants stand in a circle.

Five Gatekeepers stand at equal intervals around the circle. Vessel and Priest stand in the centre of the circle.

Gatekeepers acknowledge their sphere verbally (this consecrates the circle). They each end with the vowel sound of their sphere.

As each Gatekeeper speaks Priest installs (using Baphomet mudra) the seed mantras (through Nyasa) in the body of the Vessel. Priest and Vessel echo the vowel sound as Nyasa is done.

Once all five gates are called and installed, drumming begins (including calls of 'Zazas, Zazas Nasatanada Zazas!' and the old skool Barbaric/Enochian for those who want to say it).

Vessel kneels and is covered with cloth. Priest in centre.

Priest holds head of vessel and intones invocation:

Baphomet

CHAGLOOW YOLARM
I AM PRESENT HERE

SMERVAL TZOMDOWAH
DJ OF THE BIOSPHERE

CHURNOS COYANIOC
RAMIFY, JOIN TOGETHER

MIKURD
OPEN OUR EYES

PUZVEEP ETHENG
DO LIFE DO DEATH

EMUUL INXMAH
DO SEX WITH US

Priest raises hands to stop drumming. Baphomet singing starts.

Vessel begins to sway, move, stand. Singing stops as the Vessel adopts the Baphomet asana. Vessel declaims *The Charge of Baphomet*:

"Hear now the Word of Madness and Mystery.

I am movement and chaos, and I am the stillness inside of you. Self-born, untaught, motherless, unshakable. Giving place to no name, many-named, dwelling in fire. I am the secret Serpent coiled about to spring and in my coiling there is joy. I have made a hollow skin, from the heart of the holy tree, I compassed the earth therein, and rise from the depths of the Sea. I who am the beauty of the green earth, and the white moon among stars, the soul of nature, that gives life to the universe. I who am the taste of honey and the swirl of flies. I the dragon wing of night overspreading the earth. I Come with trumpets sounding shrill. Over the hill! I Come with drums low muttering, From the spring! I Come with flute and come with pipe! Am I not ripe? I who am a Spear that roars for blood, and a Salmon in a pool, a Lure from Paradise, and a Hill where poets walk. I am that one-pointed awareness, radiating out in all directions. From Me all things proceed, and unto Me all things must return. I call to your soul; arise and come unto me!

For 1 am the voice of the song of life, 1 am (insert names of living things, and other inspired utterances...)

1 am Baphomet!"

The Vessel wills the lingering energy into the chalice.

The Vessel offers this to the Priest who drinks. The Priest then draws the Octogram/Chaostar over the Vessel to ensure they are back to base line. The Vessel drinks and hands the chalice on, the cup passes round the circle until all have drunk.

The ritual is closed in the usual way (see end of this volume) with *From the Heights of the Heavens.*

In Praise of Made-up Religions

Chatting to a close friend recently, he noted that in contrast to a New Age "flake" that he had encountered that day, at least I "knew it was all made-up." I had to laugh! My humanist chum is well aware of my metaphysical experimentation, and his take on my belief system is that basically that I seem to believe in everything and nothing at all. Oh shit I thought, if by "believe" he means "have faith", he got the measure of me all right!

To be fair I have had a serious punt at believing something, in my case it was Christianity and frankly the psychic meltdown that eventually resulted was not pretty. Thankfully those naughty Gnostics came to my rescue. These spiritual adventurers opened my eyes to the psychological richness of metaphor and the joys of heretical rebellion. Their crazy wisdom was balm to a psyche cracking under the strain of faith and orthodoxy.

The gnostic impulse almost certainly pre-dates its pre-dominantly Christocentric expression, and reflects an understanding of humanity's struggle with belief, meaning and our experience of suffering. If you try reading the primary sources of classical Gnosticism (the Sethians, the Valentinians etc.) you can't but be both impressed and frankly bewildered by the way they engage with myth, symbol and the goal of personal liberation. The Gnostics viewed their spiritual heroes less as figures that needed to be believed in, and more as exemplars of a heightened consciousness that we should all seek to aspire to. These were gods that I actually liked rather than being required to "love"!

What drew me to them then and keeps me hooked, is the way in which revelation and insight are not the sole domain of a chosen prophet, rather it is something organic, emergent and mutating. Religious expression is seen as part of our human encounter with reality rather than something dropped out of the sky.

Avast Ye!

Even a cursory study of religious phenomena reveals both our greatest aspirations and the depths of our prejudices. Humanity's religious expressions, be it through tribal deities, anthropomorphized monotheisms or Lovecraftian terrors, all mirror our collective journey through history. This is not to imply some bleeding out of mystery; rather it glories in religion as art. The gods are real precisely because we've made them so (see Pratchett's *Small Gods* for a fantastic exposition on this concept).

Whether our inspiration is the Supernal Triad of the Kabbalah or a chthonic serpent deity, all are filtered through our beautifully human struggle. People may be drawn to more historic faiths because of their romance or track record of effective transformation but these were also just made-up, long ago, by someone really old or now dead.

While some purists may groan at my trendy preoccupation with Eris, sub-genii and other such oddities, I love the fact that the manufacturers' label is so clearly on the tin. Unlike those faiths whose claims to certainty seem shaky at best, the path of the modern gnostic explorer recognises that the map and the territory are clearly not the same. You've made that up! Yep, you've got me! It's both limited and absurd - and brilliant and a clearly heroic attempt to wrestle with the Mysteries.

Hail Eris! Pastafari!

SD

The Magickal Data Tsunami

Do you feel overwhelmed by the amount of data that is thrust in your general direction? Emails, texts, Facebook and that kind of thing. Those pesky Youtube adverts, those annoying screens at the Post Office telling you about their latest services; posters, billboards and all the rest?

I was chatting with a Sister recently and talking to her about a lecture I once attended delivered by Ramsey Dukes (Peace Be Upon Him). As part of his presentation Dukes produced two images. One of a modern day 'data warrior', some suited chap sitting in front of a bank of monitors providing him with stock exchange data, simultaneously using two telephones. This was contrasted with an image of Ramsey as a young muscular adept, standing alone in a forest glade (and looking pretty buff if I remember correctly). The point that Dukes was making with these images was that, although it looked like the stockbroker was up to his neck in information, he was in fact data impoverished when compared to our dashing young sorcerer in the woods.

In a 'natural' environment, Dukes argued, when we are seeing, for example trees, there are many more colours in the tree than might be represented on our data warrior's VDU. Then there is the way that the figure in the woods is receiving information in the form of smell, the complex sounds of the wind and of the nearby stream. There are the shifting patterns of warmth as the clouds occlude and reveal the sun. The buzzing and movement of insects, the kinaesthetic sense of the uneven earth beneath the feet...you get the picture.

My Sister and I were talking about idea in terms of psychogeography, of getting out into the landscape. We were discussing how we make ourselves sensitive through the various techniques of interacting with landscape (some of which I've written about, see *Deep Magic Begins Here...*). Being silent when we walk is one simple example. It's often pleasurable to talk as we travel in the landscape but there are undoubtedly times when it's a good move to shut up, to listen, to be receptive to the place rather than focus on expressing our internal dialogue through conversation.

Streaming vast amounts of data

As we fall silent we no longer need to attend to the narrow bandwidth of the human voice, and, since human interaction is a large part of what our brains are built for, this frees up plenty of processing power in our minds. We can then practise those lovely exercises such as seeing if one can hear five natural sounds (if walking in a rural or parkland environment) or seeing how many other conversations we can perceive (if exploring an urban space).

By becoming more open to outside impressions, basking in the complex data flow of being, as I was today beside a huge Cornish waterfall, we can open up not only our dominant senses (of sight and hearing) but we can open to the dark senses - the sense of barometric pressure, the ionisation of the air, even the scientifically measurable but (for most people) exceedingly subtle senses we have of geo-magnetism and of the lunar phase (if you want to know more about the dark senses the classic text is *The Black Goddess & The Sixth Sense* by Peter Redgrove).

A couple of days previously I was working with some academics from The University of Exeter. We were having a conversation, via Skype, with some game designers in London. When we'd done, the lecturer explained to me how she'd spent almost the whole day in her office, doing online meetings. She described how she felt 'blinkered'. Being tuned into the one channel of communication, how she'd forgotten even to eat properly that day (a half munched apple lay on her desk). Here was another example of how we get tuned in to a particular channel (in this case video conferencing) and that actually causes a reduction in the amount of information we receive (remember, food is both fuel and information). Her abandoned apple represented a loss of gustatory data in her day.

Now this isn't exactly a bad thing. Humans need to be able to focus on a given task and be persistent in their attention. Trance techniques (from drumming to TV) exist as ways to focus us even further into a very narrow band of attention.

This is useful for many things including of course many types of magickal work.

Thing is, that in entering a trance we may lose, at least for a time, our global sensitivity to our environment. We don't notice the world, and, if we do this too often, selecting only one channel of experience, we slip into information poverty.

What may seem odd then is this idea; that today many of us are actually not overwhelmed by information (e.g. all those emails) but seriously underwhelmed by it. And what's more this relative paucity of information may be the thing that may make us less sensitive to the range of environmental data that's always around us (whether we are inside or out).

There are practical consequences of this. Wikipedia teaches that after the 2004 Indian Ocean earthquake and tsunami:

> "Anthropologists had initially expected the aboriginal population of the Andaman Islands to be badly affected by the tsunami and even feared the already depopulated Onge tribe could have been wiped out. Of the six native tribes only the Nicobarese, who had converted to Christianity and taken up agriculture in place of their previous hunter-gatherer lifestyle, and mainland settlers suffered significant losses. Many of the aboriginal tribes evacuated and suffered fewer casualties."

Perhaps in the light of the suggestion above, the aboriginal people of the Andaman Islands simply had more data at their disposal and, as a result, were more sensitive to the impending disaster than their neighbours who had abandoned their traditional practices. Unlike many of the victims from elsewhere in the region 'something' told the Onge tribe to take to higher ground. I suggest this may have been because they had so much data at their fingertips in the form of a receptive engagement with the environment. They were able to notice subtle clues which, when correlated with cultural memory (of previous tsunamis) or perhaps emerging simply as gut feelings, got them out of harm's way.

So if you want to deal with your email backlog successfully, and indeed to work smarter (as they say), the best strategy is probably to go for a walk. To get out into that sea of data that is the landscape, open all the channels and max out on geosphere and biosphere bandwidth. And it may be the case that, if you want to write that article which has been in your brain for several days, you just need to go get some nature and fill up on living information. Then have some nice homecooked food, turn up the tunes and, in just a couple of hours, you can have (what I hope) are 1167 interesting words to share.

JV

Yogi Mind

"We are what we think.
All that we are arises with our
Thoughts.
With our thoughts we make the
World."

The Buddha, The Dhammapada.

Knowledge is Power apparently. At the crumbling end of this fourth aeon, our ability to use these beautiful big brains for reason, categorisation and linear problem solving is valued above all else. As we are confronted by the confusion and pain of our existence, we have sought to replace our fading myths with the Big Stories (meta-narratives) of hard science.

For Gurdjieff, the path of the mind with its intellectual and reasoning capacities was the way of the Yogi, and was the work of the "third room" or mental centre. To follow this path was to undertake the way of Jñāna yoga. As we've seen already (via the ways of the fakir and monk) in the fourth way teaching the "sly man" must integrate the best of this approach so as to pursue awakening whilst in the world.

In contrast to the path of faith, reason and the scientific method are friends to the gnostic magical practitioner. Post-Enlightenment Western Magic has tended to explore the mysterious and currently hidden via observation, reflection and experimentation. *The Book of Baphomet* brilliantly examines the genius of this approach as it vividly outlines the timeline of this bold adventure. Whether via the Royal Society, Crowley's "scientific illuminism" or the on-going forays of Chaos Magick we can see how the desire "to Know" has informed both science and Magick even if our lab coat wearing colleagues blush at our messy methodology!

Who would be foolish enough to deny how sexy and sleek science is? Here at the Blog of Baphomet we think its frickin' hot with a capital H! What our sometimes reductionist cousins need to remember is that open attitude of uncertainty and wonder that drew them to this endeavour in the first place. If the magician needs science to avoid new age naivety and intellectual sloppiness, the scientist by giving up some of their "unsafe certainty" may access those beautiful right brain insights that provide those trans-rationale eureka moments.

The mind however is not without its problems. If Buddhism acknowledges the primacy of the mind, it also acknowledges that it is with our thoughts that the problem so often lies. How is our thought content related to our experience of suffering; and how might technologies like mindfulness practice allow us to address our mental pain in a different way? While reason is a beautiful thing, sometimes as we try and think our way out of mental confusion, it feels as though we are pulling a large bundle of knotted fishing line tighter and tighter. The method of using the body and breath as a focus and gently acknowledging the arising of thought content, encourages a more lateral approach. From a place of knowing that this is all part of "monkey mind", we create the possibility of increased mental spaciousness, where we become less reactive to our thoughts and fears.

In my own life this approach to managing the mind has been critical in a number of ways. When my psyche went into meltdown as my past faith slipped through my fingers, the quiet and space that silent meditation offered provided some vital respite. Being able to hold the "observing I" position allowed me to better negotiate the core incongruence between who I felt I should have been and the person that was emerging.

For me a solid foundation in mindfulness is also critical for healthy magickal practice. As magicians, I believe that the primary spell that we cast is on ourselves in adopting the remit "to know, to dare, to will, and to keep silent". The ability to tell ourselves the story that we are magicians is the critical step in being able to shift reality - both internal and external. If we choose to work with others in our magick, part of our task is to continually re-infect each other with the meme that we can cause "change in accordance with Will."

Now while this is a vital part of the great work, the obvious danger is that we lose the ability to wake-up from the story and stand "meta" to it. To fail to do so risks grandiosity and excessive narcissism (hey we all need some self-love!). If we pride ourselves in our paradigm shifting, we also need to be able to move back to the still point of the chaos star and realise that whilst a highly effective one, chaos magick itself is also a paradigm.

Whether we describe our mindfulness practices in terms of Vipassana, Zen sitting practice or Gurdjieff's self-remembering, in order to maintain perspective and maximize new insights, such psycho-spiritual technologies are worth further lab work.

SD

Purple
I Who am All Pleasure and Purple –
Polymorphous Sex Magick

Beltane (as prolific as one should expect in both its spellings and derivations) is the season we celebrate sex. As the bluebells thrust through the leaf litter, the sun is already long in setting (at least in the British Isles). This is the time of May dances, of showers of blossom and the earnest buzzing of the bees.

Our evening of Purple magick, fortuitously coinciding with the waxing half-moon, began with a round of greetings and a banishing ritual.

Our South American Sister brings a guided visualisation. In this we strip back the blockages, imagined as a layer of slime on the skin, and emerge into our new selves. We honour what we have emerged from, for it too is part of our story. In my imagination the discarded puddle of restriction is absorbed into the earth, composting into rich soil.

Soft, oozing, fertile mud...

Following this practice is An Anointing for The Lover, each participant performing a Nyasa style placement of the bija mantras into each chakra. Marking each point with perfumed oil. A simple but powerful practice to acknowledge the sacred as expressed through our bodies.

Having thus prepared ourselves it's time for The Ardhanarishvara Brain Re-wiring Rite. Using the dual form of Shiva-Shakti we each create a sigil from that divine name and these are installed into our non-dominant hemispheres. In order to prevent unpleasantly weird physiological effects (as experienced by the developer during the alpha test of the ritual) a horizontal double-ended Shiva trident is visualised, connecting both hemispheres of the brain. We dance the sigil into our nervous systems, connecting the masculine and feminine aspects of ourselves and bringing these into unity.

The Polymorphous Elvis Transformer Ritual is next. This rides on the gnosis of the millions of orgasms which are happening across the planet right now. Moving our hips in the transgressive motion of The King and imagining the paparazzi flash-bulbs of erotic ecstasy all around us, we;

> "...key into the energy waves that are being generated, regenerated and amplified even as we sit here now. This ritual is also a tribute to Genesis Breyer P. Orridge who introduced me to the ideas of Sex Magick via the Temple of Psychick Youth and continues to break gender and push ideas of sexuality into new areas." TP808

Our sexuality, like everything else in the universe, is a flow rather than a static thing. For the closing ritual each person gets to fill in a form (and frankly, how sexy is that?). By doing so they are reflecting on how their sexuality emerges in that moment. This is done using a sexuality play spectrum chart (an example of which can be found at www.leatherati.com). We share these with each other, taking an intimate and funny moment together to disclose our (current) sexual identity in a safe space.

We sit together; silently acknowledge this intimacy, this trust. Then it's time to get up and dance (to a mix of suitable tunes); laughing and joking we step outside and light the Beltane fire, burning up the forms, the fixed notion of who we are. Realising that the ebb and flow, of on and off, is a continuous process, like sex itself; always mixing things up, stirring the genetic cauldron. And though sex can make us think of dualities - God and Goddess, male and female, wand and cup - it is actually much closer to a cloud of possibility. The erotic can, as Susan Sontag observes, erupt in a bewildering variety of expressions. Our own identities flux and flow, and even down at the genetic level things X and Y chromosomes can morph and shift, responding to hormones in different ways, and expressing themselves in a wide variety of forms.

Perhaps this is an axiom of 'Baphometic Witchcraft'; rather than a simple polarity model of sex we acknowledge that we are all, at different times and different degrees, in the flow of sexuality. Like Baphomet we are cut-up entities manifesting sex in a multiplicity of forms (including asexuality). Thus we free ourselves from the simplistic (apparently) fixed duality of forms and become something rich and strange. Our morality becomes rooted in sensitivity to issues of consent and coercion, not in a priori stereotypes of what men or women should or should not do to express their sexual nature.

The plant sex organs that are the apple blossom envelop the penetrating sisterhood of hungry honey bees. Dandelions proliferate through kinky apomixis. Horned and herm-aphroditic, snails stab love darts into each other's flesh - everything, as Austin Spare would say, fornicates all the time.

JV

Believe not that the dribbling dart of love
Can pierce a complete bosom.

Working out our Bliss

There is a view that Gerald Gardner created his version of Wicca in part to provide him with 'an excuse' to be whipped by attractive, naked young women.

This opinion is similar to the belief that Crowley's magick was really an elaborate trick for getting lots of sex and drugs. Such beliefs are understandable. We often talk about our magick as 'Work' and that word suggests something difficult, something requiring tenacity and self-discipline in the face of our natural human indolence. There is the suggestion that work is a necessary evil, a duty, and that anything that doesn't feel like toil, drudgery, and travail - just isn't proper work. Unsurprisingly in post-Protestant cultures we may assume that pleasure and delight are the antithesis of work. And therefore magickal 'work' which also happens to be something that you really enjoy or, worse, gets your rocks off, isn't proper magickal work...

Another way to think about work (in the magickal sense) is to think about the work an artist does. Certainly perspiration and practice are important to most artists, but so too is the sense that their art happens through them. The artist does their art, in part, because their muse or mental health (or as an occultist might say, their True Will) demands it. The Work of the magician is much like this, it demands to be done, and while the process may be difficult at times for both artist and magician, it may also look like play, even pleasure.

Like art, magick is about inspiration; and we are inspired by those things that stimulate us. This may range from reading a brilliant novel through to exploring ourselves through sex, drugs, ritual drama and more. It's true that the character of haughty femdom Goddess Babalon grows, in part, from Crowley's proclivities for a certain type of female lover. In this way Crowley is discovering his underlying unconscious, occult processes and projecting these outward into the world as symbols. Once the world contains the projection of his desires (for example in the form of magickal partners willing to adopt the title 'Scarlet Woman') he is able to explore his fantasy (and arguably create a space for others to realise their fantasies too). This playing out of fantasy creates a tremendous release of magickal power, sufficient, in the cases of both Gardner and Crowley, to engender new religions.

Laylah. You've got me on my knees...

The manifestation of desire in embodied terms may result in a symbolic substitution (one might channel libidinal energy into works of mathematics or painterly art - Delius for example turned his shag-monster sex life into brilliant musical composition) or may manifest in quite direct ways (as the Bacchanalian orgy). We may stylise our desires, filter them (if we are to enact them) through the mores of culture so that we ensure that individual limits are respected and meaningful consent may be given. We may dress up as Medieval Knights and re-create battles without actually killing each other, or perhaps enjoy other forms of role-play such as cos-play and Live Action Role Play.

But whatever the details of their appearance in the world occultists know the score. That which turns us on, tunes us in and lets us break out from our old selves into something bigger, deeper and, quite often, more mysterious. And of course what turns us on need not be hardcore BDSM or other 'extreme' practices; there's plenty of wisdom and playful delight to be found digging the garden or caring for injured animals. What matters is that we realise that, while magick may be 'work', this work is often best accomplished when, as mythographer Joseph Campbell advises, we 'follow our bliss'.

JV

Loosening the armour

In thinking about what we do as ritual magicians, generally we use sights, sounds, smells and sensations in order to engage the whole of our beings within the ritual space we create. By doing this we are seeking to attract those energies with which we want to work, and trying to evoke an atmosphere that is congruent with the goal of our magical endeavours. Given that we are often trying to access a state of consciousness "other" than that normally available, it seems right that effective magical work often has a sense of tension and atmosphere often induced by the sense of collective expectation.

We will all have our preferred means for getting in the zone for ritual - for me it's generally music. As the incense billows and the altar candles are lit, it's the steady throb of shamanic drumming and rattles that propels me towards the work.

Get your shaman throbbin', head out on the highway...

It might be the building tension around the beginnings of some potent spiritual work or the fact that I'm a dancing diva, but I find invariably that I have to starting moving - swaying, some gentle shaking out, or stalking around the ritual space. In his excellent *Seidways* Jan Fries describes the building of such tension as being like a boiling cauldron. Whether one chooses to explore this energy as a seething practice or channel it in a form of fluid, spontaneous movement will be determined by context and the desire of the magician.

Ecstatic dance, group shaking and psychodramatic shape shifting are but a few of the methods of exploring what's rising up in and through the body. The yogic concept of Sahaja - the natural, the simple, the spontaneous, expresses the potential sense of liberty and child-like freedom that encourages deeper exploration of these techniques. Julian has already described many of the physiological benefits of such practices but I was wondering what they might allow us to access in terms of individual and group psychology.

In trying to integrate the insights of Western psychotherapy with the methods of somatic alchemical approaches, it will come as little surprise when I name check Wilhelm Reich. As a student of Freud he was immersed in the master's insights concerning the process of ego formation and the unconscious, but like Carl Jung, Reich's own startling insights lead him to breech the confines of psycho-analytic orthodoxy. Reich primary focus was the relationship between Orgone (his term for the psycho-sexual energy that pervades the universe) and the way in which human development either enables or impedes its flow. One of his primary realizations concerned the way in which the core conditioning and defences of individuals could result in the formation of "body armour". Much of the psychotherapeutic technique developed by Reich and his followers was concerned about how body-aware approaches could be used to help soften and shift those barriers than reduce our openness and ability to connect to others.

For me, what this points towards is that technologies, such as shaking and dance, allow us to connect to the vitality and Eros of the body without having to necessarily rush towards a culturally shaped script around "having sex" or even "doing sex magick". As we connect to our body and breath, the serpentine energy of our dance allows the possibility of unlocking our inner knots. In parallel to many 'internal' martial arts, the sweating of our prayers through movement helps us to access a greater sense of openness.

In combining dance and movement with collective ritual work, I believe that we provide enhanced conditions for the further development of soul. The research of Paul Zak and other neuroscientists have documented that religious rituals and dance are both great methods for triggering the production of the neurochemical oxytocin. The production of oxytocin is associated with feeling a greater sense of closeness and attachment, more effective management of stress, and an increase in our ability to learn (neuroplasticity).

With my pointy chaos magician's hat on, I can't but help thinking about rituals making use of the Vampyre archetype and techniques experimenting with energy exchange. Although the energy invigorating us may be primarily our own, there may be sense of mutual "feeding" as the group's intent and shared exploration creates a collective atmosphere. Certainly my own experience in the group I work within, is that as we have revisited these approaches over the turning of the year there is a deepening sense of a group bodymind that is reactivated when the drumming starts and the psychonauts strut their stuff!

SD

Radical Sex, Radical Transformation

I've not long finished reading Ruth Addams excellent devotional work *A Gift of Maggots*. Ruth is the main voice in the work, though there are great contributions from other writers, notably Raven Kaldera. *A Gift...* contains poetic invocations and personal accounts, plus a decent helping of esoteric and exoteric history, about The Big B (as I like to affectionately call Baphomet).

One of the main strands in the book is the exploration of Baphomet as the deity of perverts, monsters and freaks and how in some respects this can be read as hir being the god of transgendered people, transsexuals and the disabled. This is an aspect of Baphomet that gets mentioned in *The Book of Baphomet* but *A Gift of Maggots* takes this interpretation of The Big B as its core project.

The position of trans-people in English speaking culture (transvestites, transgendered people, transsexuals) and indeed anyone who falls in some way between the (simplistic) binary duality of male and female is something that many people have worked really hard to change in the last few decades. Along with male homosexuality there have been, and are now, a wide variety of people (some trans, some not) calling for a wider cultural acceptance of the natural fact that sex and gender are fields of action rather than discrete poles.

Anyone who has spent any time exploring the area of gender fluidity, either through academic writing or personal experience, will acknowledge that physical sex (let alone the complexity of behaviour) can be a wildly diverse thing. There are all sorts of intersex, hermaphroditic and more beings who are perfectly natural outpourings of the life force on this planet (which I call Baphomet). And of course The Big B hirself is emblematic of this.

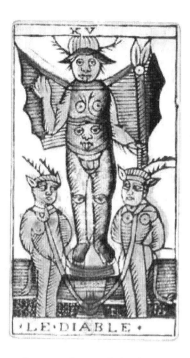

Baphomet, taking us beyond dualism since c. 1723...

A Gift of Maggots reads very well alongside Raven Kaldera's book *Hermaphrodeities* that, as the name suggests, explores the various gender fluid archetypes in mythology. In that book Raven also presents a brilliant range of interviews from all kinds of fascinating people; male to female transsexuals, female to male transsexuals, people who have been born with various intersex bodies at birth, and those who have shape-shifted through surgery and hormone pills into another form.

Slowly but surely the issue of widening gender away from just male/female is coming to the fore. I recently spoke to a Sister who was telling me about a colleague who had a child that, right from their early years, identified with the 'opposite' sex. This young person, blessed with a supportive family, had started their transition to another gender while still in the compulsory school system. What my Sister was amazed by was that, when the child returned to school with a support worker who spoke to the whole school, the child was accepted and there wasn't any bullying over that issue. More broadly there are various campaigns and organisations active in this work, such as *The International Lesbian & Gay Human Rights Commission* (www.iglhrc.org).

Such changes in culture are hard won. People have died over this issue in the same way that people died over the legalisation of male homosexuality or women's enfranchisement as citizens with voting rights.

This is why I find certain aspects of the glamorous 'outsider' mindset that some members of the esoteric community still cling to, so difficult deal with.

There's a storyline which goes something like this; we the <insert name of group> live outside of society, we're not part of the 'mainstream', we revel in our radical rejection of the status quo and (this is the clincher for me) all attempts to integrate our way of being/fucking/dressing/doing magick within wider culture are dispiriting tactics to water-down and recuperate our radicalism into the hum-drum drone of grey-face capitalist TV culture. Of course the details of the storyline will vary, but I'm sure you get the idea.

The first thing to say is that the protagonists of such views are often people who are very unlikely, because of the way they appear to others, to really be excluded from very much anything at all. So while this sense of what is, at bottom, a victim self-image may be delighted in by first world, able bodied, white middle-class men, it's unlikely that many black, disabled women in apartheid South Africa were actively happy to be full-paid up members of these 'outsider' groups.

An important a priori, within the story of those who delight in their own oppression, is that culture is a monolithic thing. Whereas, culture is, as any fule kno, a continuously morphing changing space which is actively being created at all times. Sure there can be dominant discourses (or strands, or whatever metaphor you prefer) at work, and sometimes these need to be opposed quite directly. However by conceptualising ourselves as 'the outsider' *in toto* we are not fighting but rather withdrawing from the real fray. One must either run to the hills, or go down fighting in a beautiful but ultimately pointless blaze of glory while attempting to smash The System.

In the words of Terence McKenna (Peace Be Upon Him): We're not dropping out here, we're infiltrating and taking over.

Such a position is deeply disempowering. What if gay men had been unwilling to fight for their rights but instead spent all their time wallowing in their outsider status? Speaking as a bisexual male who enjoys cross-dressing I'm really glad they stood up to be counted, if nothing else so that I can claim that identity without fear of losing my job and indeed in an environment where the law is of the land is on my side.

The outsider, the destabiliser of culture, is important, and if you read the interviews in *Hermaphrodeities*, one can see that this role is quintessentially as an agent of transformation, both of the self and of society as a whole.

Sure one might argue that things, for example modern Paganism, may get watered down when absorbed into mainstream (whatever that means these days) culture. But this is also not the whole story. Carving out the freedom to write 'pagan' on your hospital admission form is important as much for what it says about our ability to tolerate difference as it does about the perceived nature of Paganism. I pray that in the future claiming the right to use entheogens in ceremony will likewise be accepted, just as in much of the west difference in sexualities and gender forms are increasingly accepted. Social transformations can be radical and deep. Overturning the laws of Western culture about sexuality and sexual identity has been an enormous change, likewise reshaping the status of women in those cultures. This is real magic set in the real world, rather than a retreat into ancient beliefs or modern exotica, wrapped up in apocalyptic visions that would make Jehovah proud.

Cultures can certainly be bland-ified, but they can also be radically changed and become more permissive, accepting and tolerant. It's up to us, especially if we identify as witches, pagans, magicians and the like, to transform society into what we Will, and that only comes with engagement.

Not easy, but no one said The Great Work would be.

JV

Magic in the BodyMind

Recent blog posts regarding the spheres of Chaos have been prompting some reflections for me on the way that progress on the magical path might be experienced within our bodies. We might acquire new titles or embark on yet another curriculum promising new Gnostic vistas (Aeonic timeshare anyone?) but do these chunks of learning or imagined shifts in status actually translate into tangible shifts in how we experience our bodymind?

Much ink has been spilt on this blog with regards the centrality of body within our experience of this initiatory pathway that we call magic. To dance, shake and vibrate the names of god in our bodies is central to the type of ecstasy and awakening that we are in pursuit of. Ours is not a means of escaping the physical, rather the insights gained come through the messy, fragile realities of our flesh.

My own babysteps as a spiritual explorer began when I discovered a book on hatha yoga that my Mum had used whilst being pregnant with me. Much to the amusement/dismay of my working-class builder Dad, the 10 year old me spent hours trying to master "Salutation to the Sun" and crashing into furniture as I attempted daring headstands. On reflection, a big part of my love for this approach was the extent to which it demanded something of me at a very physical level. For the proto-adolescent me trying to come to terms with a rapidly changing body, the discipline and degree of bodily awareness that these exercises awakened felt deeply congruent with stirrings of the libido and the unfolding of sexual awareness.

As my body underwent the alchemical awakening of puberty, I sought to use the channels of asana, pranayama and the Maha mantra of the Vaishnavas as a means of trying to negotiate the primary challenge of "identity vs. role confusion" (cf. Erik Erickson). Eventually I chose to run into the arms of the church in hope of escaping my growing sexual uncertainty, but even here Pentecostal ecstasies found their messy way into my body via glossolalia and Holy Ghost tremblings. My own journey through Christianity and ultimately out the other side, felt as though it were a response to this deep need to experience religious sensuality as a whole body experience. Although the lives of St. Francis, St. John of the Cross and Theresa of Avila point towards such embodied ecstasies, personally I needed technologies that mapped this territory more fully.

Whilst in the early stages of training for the Anglican priesthood, the ideas of Jung turned on the lights with regards depth psychology and the potency of occult knowledge. These concepts were not abstractions, Jung's ideas concerning anima and animus flicked another switch with regards my own gender fluidity. The breadth of his engagement with alchemical traditions allowed him to develop a psychological model that contrasted starkly with orthodox Christianity. The primary dualities of light/dark, Christ/Satan that are generally viewed as oppositional, are now viewed as being polarities within which a natural oscillation can take place over time. Whether using the yogic psycho-physiology of the Ida, pingala and shushumna or the severity/mercy polarity of the Kabbalistic tree it becomes possible to dance with apparent opposites rather than struggle against them. These dualities are not mere topics for intellectual ascent, but realties that can be mapped and felt within the body.

The decision to step out onto the path of occult knowledge and magical practice is rarely an easy one to take. For me the core conditioning received via the church dictated that such a journey was psychologically and spiritually dangerous. In many senses I'd agree - the desire to eat from the tree of knowledge brings with it a process of individuation that necessitates pain and growth. Such processes ask us to examine and challenge the beliefs that we have inherited, so as to break new ground in the hope of becoming who we need to be.

As I began trying to find a path or magical tradition that made greater sense of my spiritual yearning, I became aware of how much of the body-focused material from the yogic traditions I had absorbed was resurfacing within neo-paganism. Via Theosophy, the Golden Dawn, and the work of Crowley, I came back into contact with a heady fusion of ideas that while potentially helpful, were also confusing in the lack of intellectual transparency with regards their origins. What would it look like to engage more thoroughly with the source material from which these ideas originated whilst retaining the spirit of creativity and rebellion that stirred their genesis?

Personally I have found that my own attempts to cultivate a dynamic, magically informed sadhana have provided an invaluable lens through which I can appreciate the efforts of my tantric forebears.

A Tantric forebear

My own attempts to make head-way along this path eventually led me to seek initiation within an Order that remains unapologetic about its east/west hybridism. My own initiating guru within the AMOOKOS tradition was clear in stressing many of the commonalities that exist between hermetic and tantric approaches. Given my history this has helped me greatly in seeking to integrate different aspects of spiritual explorations. Some may be uneasy about this type of approach, but for me this considered syncretism continues to contain a potentially magical dynamism.

As I walk my own path, what I find myself returning to (albeit in a number of differing traditions and sets of practices) are those methods that ask me to deepen the degree of holism in the insights that I might gain. This leaking, failing body is both the arena for potential ecstasies and the ultimate reminder of my own mortality. For me the process of alchemical refinement that I am pursuing is not one of moving up and away from the body, rather it aims to be one of return and refinement as new levels of consciousness are brought to bear.

SD

Yellow
The Still Point of the Turning World

"So the darkness shall be the light, and the stillness the dancing." From *East Coker*, T.S.Eliot *The Four Quartets*

I've recently been musing on my own use of mindfulness as it relates to my development as a magical practitioner. The idea that this practice can be used as a launch pad is not foreign to either its Buddhist or Hindu origins. This can be seen in the Buddhist use of Samatha Vipassana as a preparation for entering the deepest levels of absorption, or Pantanjali's stages prior to the experience of Samadhi. In the same way, the Western magician can be equally pragmatic as they pursue the Great Work.

The Illuminates of Thanateros in their training syllabus Liber MMM demand that the novice keep an unbroken record of their magical practice for a minimum of six months. Central to MMM is the practice of stillness and single point concentration. This seems hugely wise to my mind and perhaps reflects that at the centre of the chaos star is a still point which the magician must first develop before they can move in a direction in keeping with their Will.

In my own spiritual/magickal practice I have come to increasingly value the use of mindfulness in seeking to develop states of greater shamanic receptivity; but I think that other ways mindfulness can be utilised are manifold. A magical colleague of mine was wryly reflecting that some of his best ideas for things came to him when he was supposed to be focused on his breathing. We reflected together that the meditative state tended to allow greater access to the unconscious mind given that the usual cognitive filters were less in place.

One specific piece of work that I undertook in order to further investigate the magical use of mindfulness practice was the "Kaozen" rite. During classical mindfulness practice the practitioner seeks to maintain awareness of the breath and as distracting thoughts are noticed they are acknowledged, then let go of, so that the attention can be brought back to the breath. In contrast to this the magician in the Kaozen rite seeks to classify the material arising by mapping it onto the categories provided by the Chaos star.

Once the arising material has been noted within the 8 sub-categories of magic (Purple for sex magic, Blue for wealth magic etc., see Pete Carroll's *Liber Kaos*) then the daring psychonaut can decide how to respond to this gnosis bubbling up from their unconscious. They may choose to develop a piece of magical work as an outworking of these desires or alternately they may decide on magical activity that balances the material arising - "Hey enough of all this red war magic thinking, it's time for some green love magic!"

What this points us toward is that mindfulness practice as a weapon in the hands of the magician becomes a means for accessing and listening to the whole Self.

In the working of the Void outlined in Michael Kelly's *Apophis* he notes the key triad of Self, Desire and Outcome and the role that engaging with the Void has in shaping that desired outcome. This is a key insight in helping us listen to both ourselves and the situations we are seeking to transform; by truly attending we are more able to find the fault lines at which we can direct our energy.

In conclusion I can't help recalling the Taoist tale of Chung Tzu where a butcher with a perpetually sharp knife is asked how his blade is maintained. For him it's simple: in being attentive to the Tao (the flowing Dragon if you will), he finds the points of least resistance, where the meat seemingly falls from the bone.

In our hands Zen becomes a weapon! Seek the Mysteries!

SD

Stars of Ego Magick

The Ego often (as Rob Dickins pointed out in his brilliant presentation at the 2013 psychedelics conference in London, *Breaking Convention*) gets to be the villain of the piece. It's something to be smashed, to be transcended - it's a psychic structure that gets us caught up in petty social processes and leaves us grasping at attachments.

Yellow/Gold magick - the bright light of Midsummer time, encourages us to engage with this aspect of ourselves. What does it mean to be who we are? For this season, rather than trying to go beyond the self, let's have a respectful look at what it means to be us - right here, right now.

Golden magick

Eight people were present at our meeting, including a new participant who had predominately worked within the Ordo Templi Orientis. His presence mirrored delightfully the nature of the Work during this meeting. The Illuminates of Thanateros and OTO are quite different beasts in structural terms, but they are both, to use a rather lovely analogy, 'Organs in the body of God'. There are things the OTO structure (let alone anything to do with magic itself) allows it to do (hold public liability insurance for example) which, in certain settings can be really helpful. Meanwhile the IOT approach means that some things are trickier for that group whereas other processes (e.g. not requiring any payment of membership fees and therefore being accessible to people irrespective of their financial situation) may have benefits in other respects.

So these two Orders (as structures), unsurprisingly just like individual people, have certain things they are well suited to, and other things they find more challenging. The same is true of us as people; we're social beings and therefore while we might want a broad base of education and experience; we don't all need to be or do the same thing. And, assuming that our social relations with many others suggest we are successfully part of society as a whole, there are undoubtedly things that as individuals we should also be proud of. (Our little group is also really lucky in that not only do we have contributors from the IOT and OTO but also folk who are not part of those structures, but come from Wiccan, Zen and other backgrounds.)

Celebrating our individuality, our uniqueness, is what our Midsummer meeting was all about. This was done using a variety of techniques such as this; the *Yellow Magick Chaos Craft Ritual by me, Nikki.*

Sitting in a circle Nikki laid a packet of cigarette rolling papers and a gold pen neatly in front of her. The purpose of the ritual, she explained, was to explore our own magical names. Each person took a paper and wrote their name in gold on it. Licking the gummed edge of the paper it was then stuck on the forehead, so that each person could see the other's name (we sat in pairs).

Participants were then given the opportunity to speak to another person about the meaning of their chosen name. Each person also had a chance to listen (to a different person than the one they had explained their name to).

Following this process of explaining the naming of ourselves, and listening to the story behind the name of another, it was time to seek out a new insight from our name. To achieve this we simply take the rolling paper and crumple it up, swallowing it with a few mouthfuls of the lemon barley water from the ceremonial chalice (the sacrament used in our earlier round of introductions at the start of the meeting).

In doing this, in the style of ancient Egyptian magic, we are absorbing our name and asking for a new insight into its meaning. We sit together in a circle, each person silently repeating their own name until trance and then insight happen, guided gently by a few words from Nikki.

A simple practice like this, framed perhaps with a banishing practice and maybe a formal Statement of Intent, is sometimes all you need. The magic is in the attention the participants bring to the practice (our group members are all experienced magicians) and the skill of the ritual leader (which in the case of Ms Wyrd, having done ritual magick for quarter of a century, is considerable).

But some rituals are more about 'bells and smells', and require other paraphernalia. Other items used during this meeting included a vacuum cleaner (an underused ritual tool in my opinion, after all what do you actually use to banish stuff you don't want hanging around?), a Yellow Troll Zen teacher and internet connection to the teacher's wisdom, a composite 'exquisite corpse' creation made from three of our 'subpersonalities' (or other egos), a smoke machine, lasers, strobe lighting and the brilliant ritual music used by The Temple of Set (*Die Elektrischen Vorspiele* by *Be Not Idle In Preparation Of Thy Doom*).

For the final rite we invoked Set, the principle of the isolate intelligence, the separate sense of self and of being-in-the-world. Then, emerging from the darkness into the light of the sun god Ra, we each put on an outfit we'd brought especially for the purpose. There were sharp suits, feathered masks, leopard print high heels, gold body paint and much more besides! There was dancing, mutual admiration and a photoshoot!

Stars in their eyes

Celebrating our unique individuality and ourselves is something that, particularly perhaps in Britain, people get uneasy about. We don't want to seem big headed; which is fair enough. However we need to recognise that it's okay to celebrate in this way, and that to big ourselves up doesn't mean we have to put someone else down. Quite the reverse - in fact, as my OTO Brother might remark; 'Every man and every woman is a star'.

JV

Picture of the gold chaosphere pendant courtesy of the maker, Russell Lownsbrough.
http://www.whaleandsmith.co.uk/

Cutting up the Ego

I was recently reading the biography of a pagan teacher on their blog and was interested in the way in which their self-description had shifted over the several years that I'd been interested in what they were up to. While they had initially sought to emphasise their pedigree in the witchcraft tradition they had trained in, in recent times they had ceased calling themselves a pagan as a result of exploring types of mysticism that emphasised non-dual forms of awakening. On my most recent visit they seem to have moved yet again, to a place where the witch and transcendentalist seem to be on better terms with each other!

Biography and self-identification are fascinating processes. On this blog the three main contributors have tried to pin down a number of descriptors that seek to provide a window into an aspect of who they are. Whatever semiotic sign that we choose to adopt, we are trying to communicate some sort of meaning to someone (even if that's primarily ourselves) at a given moment of time. These attempts at self-definition are magical acts in and of themselves. As we are buffeted by the multiplicity of roles and demands that life places on us, the act of calling forth an aspect and giving it a name requires both self-understanding and will. Whatever the tribal affiliations that they may or may not indicate, their value is unlikely to be permanent especially if you engage in the type of transformational practices that seem to amplify the pre-existing forces of impermanence and entropy.

Julian recently flagged-up a fantastic interview from 1974 between William Burroughs, and the Ziggy Stardust era David Bowie. In the interview Bill and Dave provide us with some brilliant insights as to how these adept magician/ artists engaged with the idea of the self:

"Burroughs: They try to categorize you. They want to see their picture of you and if they don't see their picture of you they're very upset. Writing is seeing how close you can come to make it happen, that's the object of all art. What else do they think man really wants, a whiskey priest on a mission he doesn't believe in? I think the most important thing in the world is that the artists should take over this planet because they're the only ones who can make anything happen. Why should we let these fucking newspaper politicians take over from us?

Bowie: I change my mind a lot. I usually don't agree with what I say very much. I'm an awful liar.

Burroughs: I am too.

Bowie: I'm not sure whether it is me changing my mind, or whether I lie a lot. It's somewhere between the two. I don't exactly lie, I change my mind all the time. People are always throwing things at me that I've said and I say that I didn't mean anything. You can't stand still on one point for your entire life."

Burroughs and Bowie are on record as having been involved in occult practice, and both of them exemplify the type of continual reinvention and conscious image manipulation that one might associate with the spirit of contemporary culture. Both also made extensive use of cut-ups as a way of loosening the hold of linearity in relation to art and communication. Like collage, cut-ups seek to use existing material in new ways that often involve the combining and juxtaposition of words and images so as to create new insight and meaning.

In tracking the lineage of cut-ups as an approach, from the surrealism of the Dadaists, Brion Gysin, Burroughs and Genesis P-Orridge, we can begin to see the depth of magical thinking embedded in this technique. As we seek to engage with and manipulate reality, the cut-up not only embodies the desired efficacy of our sorcery, but also the fluid shape-shifters that our arte forces us, the magicians, to become. If our magic has any real depth, then our ego must undergo a similar process of reassembly.

Magical cut-up

The ego so often gets a bad press in spiritual circles, but often it simply represents our habits and attempts at self-protection as we encounter the pain and challenges associated with the rough and tumble of making sense of life. Such pain by necessity generates defences and the development of psychic armour. These are not bad, in and of themselves, but they can become problematic if we wish to evolve and awaken the deeper, more mysterious aspects of Self. If we become over-identified with the armour, then we might be in danger of forgetting about the lithe athlete that lives within!

Magick cuts us up. It often parallels so-called mental illness in fracturing the crusty shell of ego so that the light of Self can bleed through the gaps. We need to remain sensitive to the pacing of such work so that we allow the development of new, more flexible ways of being, without feeling overly exposed. Such work necessitates compassion towards the self as we bow in thanks to the function of the ego, in helping us survive and negotiate the competing needs within us. Perhaps never fully abandoned, the ego becomes an effective tool for the awakening Gnostic explorer.

Whilst recently reading Mark Cunningham's *The Hours* I came across this fabulous description of the way in which the mysteries of self can interact for the artist. In describing the process of Virginia Woolfe he writes:

> "This morning she may penetrate the obfuscation, the clogged pipes to reach the gold. She can feel it inside her, an all but indescribable second self, or a parallel, purer self. If she were religious, she would call it the soul. It is more than the sum of her intellect and her emotions, more than the sum of her experiences, though it runs like veins of brilliant metal through all three. It is the inner faculty that recognizes the animating mysteries of the world because it is made of the same substance, and when she is very fortunate she is able to write directly through that faculty."

Within the schema of the chaos star the work of ego magic is associated with yellow magick and the warmth of the midsummer sun. As the solstice approaches (at least for those of us north of the equator!) may our magics aid the shedding of old skins that inhibit the potential of what we might become.

SD

Science of the Soul

'What is the relationship between psychology and modern magic?' was a question asked of me by a friend recently. There are many ways one could look at that relationship. There is the broad historical relationship between magic (as 'natural philosophy') and science in general. There is the general point that psychology is literally the study of the soul and therefore one might argue that ancient and modern religious and esoteric thought has always had something to say on these matters. One might alternatively look at the uneasy relationship between modern experimental (often laboratory based) psychology and psychoanalysis.

But, if we stick to the terms of the question in that it's 'modern magic' we're interested in, we can explore what I think may be the underlying assumption; that magic is a specialist form of applied psychology. Frater U.D. famously defined a series of magical paradigms here in the form of the spirit, energy, psychological, information and meta models. Although many of the principles that Frater U.D. ascribes to the psychological model are perhaps more properly thought of as psychoanalytic, he does, in my view, correctly suggest that this model has been the favourite of English speaking magicians, especially since the 1970s. Chaos magic usually considers the 'core technology' of magic to be belief-shifting and gnosis, and both these principles can be most readily understood as psychological processes rather than the activities of spirits or energy. In this essay the author hints that beyond the traditional chaos magic twin-pillars of belief/gnosis there lies the information model that does not rely on trance techniques and (like anything new) is double-plus good. He also mentions the meta-model, which is pragmatic utilitarianism, and when it comes down to it, is how many magicians engage with their practice.

My own view is that psychological understanding is a major component in the ontological field within which modern magic takes place. It's the basic cultural landscape in which our rituals and practices happen. Even people that are adopting a highly spiritist model of magic (and this seems, of late, to have become terribly fashionable) must perforce live in a world where psychology is 'the Daddy' now. Our language is shot through with Freudian, Jungian and Skinnerian terminology. Our world is governed by an awareness of human psychology; in advertising, in law and even in those little details of life like the fact that your ATM gives the card back first rather than dispensing your money for (psychologically) obvious reasons. Psychology as a science continues the de-centring process that has been critical in the narrative of the post-Medieval world. In astronomy once we realised that Earth goes round the Sun we lost our position in the centre of the cosmos. Once we understood evolution, we lost our place as the pinnacle of God's creation; and became just another animal. Once we began to appreciate that there is both consciousness and then there are all those unconscious processes at work, even our self-awareness was knocked off centre stage.

For magicians this de-centring of the self isn't such a big problem as we tend to have a much bigger definition of 'self' than the narrow sliver of waking awareness we call consciousness. I heard a lecture from Michael Staley (of The Order formally known as the Typhonian OTO) a couple of years ago, where he pointed out that magic was a process where the unconscious 'tides' were more important than (conscious) will. He suggested that magical acts only really work when they are what the unconscious wants and that the wise magician pays attention (as far as one can to unconscious phenomena) to these tides and attempts to swim with them. For any magickal operation, said Mr Staley, there is the possibility of it working, or not working, or of working in reverse. Pointing out that you'd never use a gun that behaved like this, he suggested that most magick should be about listening to the unconscious and doing its will.

In many ways this is what Crowley was going on about with his idea of True Will. Putting aside the more metaphysical interpretations of the Will, Crowley was interested in enacting one's unconscious drives. His idea was that, unfettered by social restriction, the unconscious would well up, turning every man and woman into a genius, driven by his or her daemon (in the classical sense), and everything would be groovy. Reason was 'a lie' and 'Because' was 'accursed'. The apparent naivety of this proposal can be forgiven when we consider that Crowley lived in a world of Victorian prudery, hypocrisy and Freudianism. He understandably imagined that the suffocation of the choking strictures of social convention were what was holding us back from a Golden Age. No wonder he is one of the 'people we like' in the famous montage for Sgt. Pepper's Lonely Hearts Club Band and the hero of the radical 1960s.

Today we might take a more nuanced view. Aided by the fantastic breakthroughs in neurology, and decades of brilliant experimental psychology, we now have a much better idea of how humans really work. And, while we may still use terms like left and right brain, introvert and extrovert etc, most of us admit to a much more complex and indeed malleable model of the psyche, especially in relation to the social environment.

This malleability is where magic comes in. As well as understanding better how our minds work, we have also gone on to develop many more ways of changing them. The number of therapeutic systems which psychology has provided are legion (even if we only stick to those considered 'mainstream'). As agents of change these techniques are magical in that they allow us to change how we see the world and thus (at the very least, in a subjective sense) the world itself. Psychology, especially experimental psychology, represents one of the best approaches we have to mapping ourselves, and by having better maps we can better determine where we want to (or can) be. (And of course educate ourselves in how others may wish to use these tricks to change our minds for us.)

There is nothing at all wrong about familiarising oneself with ancient maps of the soul, whether it is the Qabalah, the Nine Worlds or something else that tickles your fancy. But the modern magician should also be familiar with some of the key findings of experimental psychology. Certainly a familiarity with psychoanalytics is essential to understand the work of Crowley, Fortune, Grant, Spare et al. It's also essential to appreciate some of the most interesting and innovative deployments of magic in the modern age. These include such gems as the *Psychomagic* of Alejandro Jodorowsky or those brilliant Temple of Psychick Youth videos with Derek Jarman.

So rather than see psychology as a retreat for magic, a sad admission that 'it's all in our heads', we can instead appreciate it as providing a wonderful new cartographic tool that, in only just over a century, has thrown up a wide variety of technologies for the discerning magician. It's also, whether we like it or not, the language of the modern (post) industrialised age. As magicians, if we are to be empowered in this world, we must know how to speak this language fluently.

JV

Headology

I've got a friend who has a PhD in brain science (in fact she's an MD too so all those 'Doctor, Doctor...' jokes are perfect). Her work involves scanning people's brains to help us understand how memory functions. She once told me that she and her colleagues spent an entertaining few weeks replacing the word 'mind' with 'brain' in their daily speech. 'Brain the gap' is therefore the message one hears on alighting from a London underground train. 'I just can't get it out of my brain' for that irritating/catchy tune. 'Brain out!' as an injunction to increase attention, or 'brain over matter' when discussing the paranormal.

Within esoteric and psychological sciences there is a group of similar practices. There is E-Prime, which removes the verb 'to be' to create a language that emphasizes process rather than (apparently) static states. Then there is Crowley's injunction to remove the word 'I', which he recommends (along with a bit of Emo style self-harm) to his students during his sojourn at The Abbey of Thelema, and of course a whole battery of techniques from NLP.

All these processes make us more vigilant and can have far reaching effects on our world-views.

So, with this in mind (or brain), I'd propose a little chaoist variation. Take one of your beliefs and find a way of modifying your language to suggest that your normal assumptions about it may not be the case. The example I'm particularly thinking of would be when we say that we've met such-and-such an entity in spirit work. Or when we've invoked a God or Goddess, or been travelling in spirit vision. In all these cases 'in my brain' may be added.

For instance:

"I met the jaguar spirit and it spoke to me - in my brain'.

'The Goddess was invoked into the High Priestess and I could really see the energy - in my brain'.

'The Loa are really powerful - in my brain'.

'I've spent many years working with a series of awesome demons - in my brain'.

Of course one might argue that such statements are just the natural return and re-valuing of the spirit model into our culture. I'd agree with that and say that it's certainly sometimes important to think in this way:

Jung had a very disturbed patient who claimed to have been on the moon. Not that she thought this to be a conscious reality; it was a dream in which she travelled to the moon. Jung reported years later to analyst Marie Louis von Franz that his patient had indeed been on the moon. In a well-known interview with this remarkable first generation analyst, von Franz commented that when Jung told her that his patient had really been on the moon, she thought that Jung was crazy. She was very rational and thought that for Jung to say that the girl had "really" been on the moon was not reasonable. And indeed, normal rationality fails in these cases.

In a world that one might argue is dominated by reductionist discourses the spirit model serves to re-empower our subjective imagination. But the point for me is that we don't need to throw the materialist baby out with the bathwater. Instead we should attempt to include the spirit world in our material world. Rather than replacing one language with another, we should be seeking to broaden our vocabulary. We acknowledge the metaphorical truth of the world both internal (subjective experience) and external (our sense data, including that collected by scientific investigation).

So the miraculous fact that our minds can interact with spirit entities may be described in terms of invisible imaginative worlds, and also as brain events. We know this to be true because we've got a range of chemicals and even magnetic helmets that can induce the experience of meeting entities. Hardly remarkable since our senses give us the impression of meeting conscious entities (people) every day. So saying the 'astral' (which in a proper Santo Daime style should be pronounced 'ass-traal') is in our brains is nothing more than a statement of fact. Everything is in our brains and, while in a metaphysical sense we could talk about the non-local nature of consciousness and all that, a brain would seem to be an important part of the equipment. People who think otherwise could perhaps demonstrate the strength of their conviction in non-brain mediated consciousness by removing theirs (with one of those nose pickers the ancient Egyptians used on the dead perhaps?) and then attempting to go down the shops to buy ten fags.

The use of 'in my brain' also serves to remind us of the uncertainty of our perceptions and the fact of their partiality. I may have seen something nasty in the triangle but I saw it from a specific perspective, at a specific time and so on. Maybe such a practice would put the brakes on all those folk who spend their time conjuring spirits from the vasty deep and then banging on about their visions. Of course were I being handsomely paid like Jung I'd be happy to listen to it all, but since I'm not I often feel these stories demonstrate that speaker has become locked into one 'reality tunnel' (as Leary would say).

Entering a relationship with a spirit can be a powerful magic. But to be a magician is to be able to see that relationship in many ways, including as a brain event. Seeing things as neurological processes does not have to be disempowering. Seeing clinical depression as having a neuro-transmitter component is factually accurate. It can provide us with medicines to help people and is emphatically not identical with ignoring the environment in which the depressed person is living. Understanding the brain mechanics of mental illness isn't about forgetting social, cultural, dietary and other factors in its aetiology.

If we are to re-enchant the world then we must include all our understanding of it and not take refuge in what can be an egocentric, subjective, imaginal world. We should open ourselves out to many languages and many perspectives. Sometimes we should speak of the spirit of the mushroom, at other times of its chemistry, of its cultural history and its mythic meaning. And whichever language we use could always aim to contain a destabilizing element within our descriptions. Something that serves to open us up to other interpretations and remind us of the limits of what we think we know - in our brains.

JV

Intensify the normal

As magicians we should aim for at least one ecstatic moment each day. This of course doesn't mean that a day without some full-on practice is a day wasted. For Austin Spare, Peace be Upon Him, those occultists who limit their magic to symbolic acts within ceremony are missing out. "Their practices prove their incapacity, they have no magic to intensify the normal, the joy of a child or healthy person, none to evoke their pleasure or wisdom from themselves."

Morning river

I am located in this landscape. I know its history and its people. I have my own memories, joyful and painful, located in this place. My breath is easy and I find myself stopping for a moment by the quay and looking out towards the old shipyard and beyond to where my river curves round to meet her sister (the river Taw) as together they unite with the sea.

I am, for a moment, transported into that hyper-reality which always, on reflection, makes me think I've stepped into a frame from a graphic novel. There is a razor sharpness to my senses and I am both observer and at one with the world I inhabit. I feel profoundly grateful that I am able to experience this moment.

Just before I go into the gallery where I'm working, I notice how the grass beneath my feet bends. I've deliberately walked off the path in order to enjoy this sensation.

Yes, all our ceremonial work, our yoga and study matters - but only if it increases our capacity to enjoy the normal that bit more.

JV

Red
Curses, Invocations - The tactical deployment of Red War Magick

The first iteration of our Chaos Craft Wheel of the Year ends with Lammas, the festival of the cutting of the corn. In my landscape this is around the time of the first grain harvest. Red fruits appear (in my garden that means cherries, raspberries and red currants). When I was a kid in Hertfordshire this was also the time of burning the fields. The sky would darken with the smoke of smouldering stubble, and we would occasionally gather at the edges of the fields and race the flames as they ate their way across the blackened earth.

Burning down the house

Lammas is the time for cutting, for breaking, for reaping and engaging with the necessary destructive elements of our cultures, the cosmos and ourselves. We prune back the summer growth, and burn what is no longer needed.

For our Red Magick meeting to begin we acknowledged our group's inspiration from The Craft, passing around a chalice of red wine as our introduction. This wine had first been consecrated as the living witch-blood, an evocative idea that turns up in the Cultus Sabbati material and in that awesome grimoire *Mastering Witchcraft* by Paul Huson. We each hand the cup round the circle, drinking with the words 'my blood' and offering to the next participant with the words 'your blood'. Bound by this symbolic blood pact we enter an evening of Red rites.

Curses are tricky beasts and worth considering before we rush in, wands blazing. Who do we curse and why? Of course even to swear at someone is a curse. In that situation, by the visceral power of taboo words, we may attempt to harm, to upset. In more explicitly magickal contexts we may try all kinds of operations; against individuals, against organisations, against ideas. When we consider curses we need to think deeply about what we're doing.

In a Chaos Magick group on Facebook I recently responded thusly to someone who was asking if members thought it was cool to curse someone who'd pissed them off:

"When considering curses, of which of course there are many types (and indeed any act of magick), I'd suggest that you contemplate what the ritual/approach will do to you. "Battle not with monsters, lest ye become a monster, and if you gaze into the abyss, the abyss gazes also into you." like Nietzsche says. Consider how you can act to increase compassion, transformation and healing in the situation rather than the violence and distrust that has motivated your thoughts. This more subtle approach might help you not get trapped in a 'me vs. them' dichotomy and is likely to leave you more empowered rather than less. You'll also undoubtedly win. ☺"

So the curses we laid on our night of Red Magick were not against people, but aimed at the transformation of certain situations. This is delicate magick. The injunction not to 'Battle with Monsters' from Nietzsche doesn't mean not to do anything, where there is a problem we should address. Rather it points to the idea that if you demonise your opponent you run the risk of becoming like them or of losing your own humanity.

There are certainly situations that demand our opposition, but we as magicians must be intelligent in this, and use our Skilful Means when faced with these difficulties. Lots can be learnt from writers such as Sun Tzu and Miyamoto Musashi. (The quote of Sun Tzu's *The Art of War,* "Build your opponent a golden bridge to retreat across." has great relevance, at the time of writing, in terms of proposed military intervention in Syria. But that, as they say, is another story.)

Of course a curse against the project of fracking in the British Isles, for example, isn't a curse necessarily against any particular person. It's against a method for extracting energy from the earth that is supported by a series of very short-sighted values and intentions. Naturally this type of Work must also combine with supporting the various other levels of opposition to these projects. In that moment we summoned the dragon to rise up, through the land and the people, to oppose fracking. Of course the earthquake the next day could have been 'just coincidence', and the announcement by prospecting firm Cuadrilla, that they might be on unsafe ground legally to continue their work (pun intended), might simply be 'one of those things'. We certainly did not 'cause' these events, however our magick was part of the network of Wyrd (of actions by many people at many levels) that, for the moment, has resulted in this company withdrawing its application for more drilling.

A naive view is to imagine that Cuadrilla is 'the enemy' and that the enemy is bad, not 'of us', something we must destroy. Whereas in fact by acknowledging our connection (if nothing else as energy consumers) to what we oppose, we find our own power.

After an evening of several Red rituals where else can you go with the playlist but to a little Petro Voodoo? Asking for the presence of the Loa, dancing and chanting we enter the space of war, of violence, of conflict and again look for the transformative potential of these most difficult experiences.

Here in our underground temple we deploy a technique from the Feri Tradition of Craft. We bow before our enemies, for they remind us of what we hold dear. We acknowledge that they remind us that there are many views of reality. We bow before them as they inspire us towards greater compassion and creativity. We bow before them and remind ourselves that we are fighting for them and their children, and in doing so became stronger in the Work that we do.

Back from the underground, our final act of Red Magick isn't a curse but is still about breaking stuff; this time obstacles. Ganesha's favourite colour is red and, while he's (mostly) a jolly god that likes sweets, he's also a fierce ally. Making our 108 salutations to this gigantic, powerful deity we transform the Red of War into the living Red of healthy, circulating blood; our witch-blood, my blood, your blood. As we say in the Chaos Craft: "From the heights of the heavens, to the depths of the earth, we are one heart - connected. Blessed Be."

JV

*Final Red Magick spirit jar filled with ash from our rituals.
Jai Ganesha!*

The Cutting of the Corn

Last week I was asked to do a Naming Ceremony, one of those lovely, approachable and inclusive Pagan events. Rather than being for an infant the ceremony was at the request of a young woman. She asked me be Priest for the rite; which was perhaps closer to a Confirmation (in the Christian tradition) than anything else.

For these kinds of things I like to have a sense of the movements, the key acts within the ritual, and rarely do I use any written script. I asked Mum if she would tell us all (there were about 40 people at the ceremony) what name she had chosen for her daughter. Then I was able to ask (since she wasn't a baby) if her daughter would accept her name (she did).

After a blessing with the four elements I asked the younger brother of the girl being named to come forward. I reminded her that one day she too would be an ancestor, would be the care giver to others (even as she cared for her brother as his older sibling) and perhaps one day (like the people standing around her) she would be parent or guardian to a child of her own.

Travelling to the other side of the island a couple of days later with my children I was able to spend some time with my parents. I was struck by how my Dad, although still a very lively man, is getting old (he's 75). In the light of my own words at the Naming ceremony I became deeply aware that it is quite probable that in a few years' time he will become one of the Ancestors (with a capital 'A') and I will become the oldest male in my immediate family.

These realisations dawn on me, on us, and so we feel ourselves as part of the flow of existence. As I've started work with the

Chaos Wheel of the Year model I've been linking this process with the phase between Midsummer (yellow magic) and Lammas (red magic). In this system we (that is me and Frater Pelagius) have been exploring the idea that each of the eight sectors of the Wheel relate to a phase of life. Midsummer to Lammas relates to the period from our 40's until our 50's. During this phase we find ourselves fully mature and part of this maturity is about the cutting down (the red magick process) of our parents. They fall like the Lammas grain, they are harvested into the Ancestral realm.

The Chaos Wheel of the Year - showing the decades of life that may be explored in each sector

When we are babies we are born into the on-going play of life. Gradually we pick up the script, start to improvise our own lines. When our parents leave the stage, responsibility to continue the script (and of course, a new phase in our power to amend it) falls to us.

In practice this point on the wheel reminds us (whatever age we are) to be mindful of the process where we must separate ourselves from others, from our parents (when we are born, when we are named, and when they die). It also reminds us that this separation isn't about rejection but is a necessary condition to transformation. The song of John Barleycorn expresses this beautifully, where the violent assaulting of little Sir John by the farmer, the miller, the brewer is essential for his transformation into 'the strongest man at last'.

So here's to separation as a process that is essential to our transformation as magicians, as individuals. Not rigid isolation but a flow that is punctuated by moments of revelation and renewal.

JV

Spiritual Knighthood

The challenge to find meaning in the midst of our lives can at times feel as elusive as a search for the Grail. Not only are we struggling to find out the location of such a desired relic, but we are also troubled by the suspicion that we are not sure whether we would recognise it if we did stumble upon it! In the midst of such uncertainty it can be tempting to abandon the quest as we feel overwhelmed by the multiplicity of paths on offer, and their competing truth claims.

The desire to take up such a quest often indicates the beginnings of our awakening. As our dissatisfaction with the 'answers' provided by family and society grows stronger, the hero within needs to separate themselves from the anaesthetising effect of such dominant discourses. Some will be upset by our distancing behaviour and others may rage at our rebellion, but when we feel the inner-flames of purpose ignite, we know that psychic atrophy will result if we fail to pay heed to such stirrings.

I have recently been reading Lindsey Clarke's excellent modern adaptation of Wolfram Von Eschenbach's *Parzival*, and within I have found deep wells of insight for those of us seeking to cultivate spiritual heroism. In the tale, Parzival's mother seeks to protect her son from the demands of the world and the allure of knighthood by keeping him in a state of naive ignorance. When he eventually meets three knights from Arthur's court, he is so overwhelmed by their radiance, that he mistakes them for Gods. He is awakened by the brilliance of the sun reflected upon their armour and even the grief of his mother fails to divert him from his desire to pursue his destiny.

This idea of spiritual knighthood is an interesting one in that it offers helpful paths of transformation while also being fraught with dangers if not understood with considered subtlety. History is strewn with examples of groups and misguided individuals who have used the martial, combative focus of the knight in an externalised fashion. The recent horrors in Norway at the hand of Anders Breivik provide a sobering example of what happens when concepts of 'honour' and 'defence' are appropriated by the fearful or psychopathic. If we fail to see that our sword strokes need to focus on our own ignorance, then we may be prone to projecting our fear of ourselves onto some scapegoated 'other'. Some may feel that the martial focus of knighthood is innately unhelpful, but it could be argued that our need to both attack and defend are so primal, that we need a means for transforming such desires.

Whom does it serve?

As Parzival journeys along the road he finds that his certainties and self-perception are repeatedly challenged, as he seeks to find the meaning of true knighthood and what it might mean to be worthy of the Grail. When he begins his quest, the literal and the masculine provide him with benchmarks for how he should be in making sense of his universe. His first guru, Gurnemanz, is more than adept in teaching him the use of the lance and shield, but when considering matters of the heart and deep pain he is sadly lacking. It is this stiff upper-lip, don't ask questions attitude that causes his initial failure when confronted by the wound of the Fisher King.

In keeping with the longings of the troubadours and the idealisations of courtly love, Von Eschenbach views the embrace of feminine wisdom as being critical in the transformation of our hero. The story of Parzival is full of wise female voices, and his struggle to integrate their insights is central to his endeavour to become a true Grail knight. Such transformation can be a far from gentle process as Parzival encounters women as wise-equals rather than as a protective mother. When he seeks to minimise his initial failure at the Grail castle, his cousin Sigune's reproach of him opens up a sense of despair that drives his initiatory purpose deeper.

This process of seeking balance and necessary complexity is mirrored within the development of Tantric and Sufi traditions at similar points in history. The parallels between these traditions and the Grail mythology could be framed as a shared emphasis on psychological alchemy and a more nuanced understanding of gender roles. Time, hardship and mimetic evolution may have led to the development of gender identities that are increasingly subtle and congruent with our inner yearnings, but I believe that the validity of these stories remain as expressions of how the dance of perceived polarity gets worked out.

In the same way that Parzival must contend with the repeated deconstruction of his self-perception as a knight, so his understanding of the divine must be abandoned and reborn.

Parzival must take leave of his naive perception of how God intervenes in the world and embrace an apparently dark world where he walks alone. He must move from his child-like certainties and embrace the adolescent energy of the adversary. Only as he exercises the existential bravery of staring into the void can he begin to experience the numinous in a new way. Sitting with the mystery, the Runa, and letting it speak to our own depths in its own terms may feel challenging, but the pursuit of true knighthood will allow little else.

I don't want to completely spoil the ending, but it behoves me to observe that as the Grail itself represents something at once subtle and mysterious, while holding great powers of healing, so the very pursuit of it seems to demand the development of such qualities in its seeker. In these times of existential confusion, the development of our own internal poise can feel like one of the few means of making headway. Even if old certainties no longer ring true and we feel driven on by the longings of our souls, we can still walk a path of spiritual heroism: Here, we acknowledge the limits of our knowledge and yet still choose to live and act in good faith.

SD

A Little Off-Balance

"This expression of the I Ching reveals the dynamic magick of AMOOKOS. The Ridgepole is the fluid yet equipoised point existing between the two states of active/passive" Shri Lokanath, *Tantra Magick* p93.

Quite a few of the spiritual traditions that I personally find helpful as a magician have the concept of balance at their heart. Within the vast array of Buddhist traditions, the concept of the 'middle way' is generally recognised as embodying the aspiration of steering between the excesses of either forceful asceticism or indulgence. The Etz Chayim or 'Tree of Life' within the Kabbalistic schema contains the 'middle pillar' that sits between the black/white, male/female polarities of severity and mercy. Within Hindu Tantra, the Shushumna, the central channel of tantric psycho-physiology, sits between the solar/lunar opposition of the Ida and Pingalanadis. Each of these traditions contains their own unique religious languages, which defy over-simplification or homogenisation, but there seems to be a shared goal of seeking a way between apparent polarities.

Both philosophy and religion have sought to observe and communicate something of the natural oscillation between primal polarities. In Taoism we have the notion that when something becomes either too Yin or Yang then inevitably the movement will begin towards the other. For Hegel every idea, or thesis, would inevitably have its opposite antithesis. The tension between these two poles eventually produces a middle position or 'synthesis' as reconciliation of these ideas. This synthesis then becomes its own thesis and so the dance continues!

Odinist pole action...

In thinking about such middle-ways, one wonders if there's a danger that we could end up either endlessly compromising or winding up with some kind of bland centrism. What might it actually mean to work with balance and why does it seem to be such a frequently reoccurring motif within esoteric work? Over at the Zen and Northern Mysteries blog *Odin the Wanderer,* I recently attempted to reflect on the rune Dagaz as a specifically heathen manifestation of this mystery:

"In meditating on the rune "Dagaz" over a number of years it is one of those runes that has taken on a huge significance for me as an emblem of spiritual aspiration. Personally I experience its essence as an expression of the twilight reality that exists in between light and darkness. For me it embodies the realm of the magician-shaman par excellence. As we "walk between the worlds" it is inevitable that we encounter that liminal knife-edge where polarised certainties either breakdown or are sustained in dynamic tension.

When I gaze at Dagaz, my eye is naturally drawn to the point of connection between the two triangles - am I travelling down a hall to some distant far-point, or am I at the aperture of a side-on hour glass where time travels from past to future? Dagaz invites me to dwell in the "now" that is the point in between.

This idea of a third reality that sits in between two apparent opposites has a real basis within the heathen tradition that goes beyond a borrowing of the Taoist "Yin Yang", or the Kabbalistic "middle pillar". Northern lore is strewn with sacred threes; Fire, Ice and the universe created in the tension between its polarity, the Norns, the three aspects of Odinn, the Valknut, the nine worlds (3×3), and so the list goes on.

To engage with Dagaz is to become aware of these dynamic tensions and the potentiality that exists in working in this third place.

What I don't wish to imply is that heathenry advocates some kind of endless compromise. When we mark the turning of the year, we are seeking to acknowledge a movement away from the sun and back toward it as the year passes through the seasons - an oscillation, if you will. Dagaz invites us to acknowledge polarity and to engage in a dance with it!"

So we're backing to dancing again - the flow of the body as it moves in response to the music - subtle adjustments and micro-movements as weight shifts from one foot to another. To be 'in balance' rarely entails a 50/50 split, often it seems to be more about staying on one's feet as we seek to channel the ecstasy rising up.

Magick is often the conscious induction of instability in order to create change. These are technologies that are designed to plunge elbow deep into your unconscious and give it an almighty stir. As much as results magick might produce quantifiable change 'out there', it seems undeniable that the major locus of magickal activity and change is 'in here': "in consciousness according to Will" (Dion Fortune). If it's stability you're seeking, stay away from religious and spiritual traditions that have a major magickal component (and that's most of them) - you're only going to upset/unbalance yourself.

As dancers in the Great Work we balance, unbalance and re-balance as we use our Magick to keep moving and shake out any signs of psychic atrophy. For me the goal of balance seems to be less about pursuing some safe middle-ground, and more about cultivating the poise to move how and when we need to.

SD

The Ninth Gate...

In reading through the array of differing topics and concerns that have been addressed via this blog, one of the oft-repeated themes is that of contemporary mindfulness practice. For many of its contributors, the use of these meditative techniques provides a potent means for synthesising the competing agendas within our everyday lives.

In the schema laid out during the Chaos Craft project, the magicians participating sought to shape their own experimentation so that it mapped more harmoniously onto the turning of the year's wheel. During the shifts in climate, daylight and nature associated with these changes, our magical practice also morphed as it sought to mirror varying degrees of either surging outwards or retreating back. While the re-orientating of the colours of chaos has allowed a sense of greater congruence between our activity and its natural context, we have still found great value in a more conscious use of stillness practices. Whichever arrow of the chaos-star we found ourselves working with, we often felt the need to return to the still-point at the star's centre. This still-point provides us a 'Ninth Gate' of practice.

What follows is a brief reflection on some of the potential benefits connected with mindfulness practice. While these may not seem overtly occult in nature, in my view they are profoundly magical in seeking to engage with the deepest aspects of our humanity.

Personal Benefits:
It seems a somewhat obvious thing to say, but many of us live our lives very quickly, bombarded by information, struggling to get our bearings in a world that seems to be ever changing. If nothing else mindfulness practice provides us with a chance for stillness, a chance to slow down. With more mental space

at our disposal our ability to truly listen and therefore to learn takes on a radically different quality.

What mindfulness allows us to do par excellence is create a sense of distance between ourselves as thinkers. and the thoughts we have. The popularity of this practice in the field of psychological therapies is largely based on the gentle manner in which it allows the practitioner to notice their thoughts that arise. The approaches of Mindfulness-Based Stress Reduction (MBSR) and Mindfulness-Based Cognitive Therapy (MBCT) both recognise that our response to thoughts and emotions as they arise is critical in terms of the impact that they have on us.

The evolution of these therapeutic models has highlighted the possibility, that the spirals of negative thinking so familiar to those with reoccurring depression can be questioned. For the mindfulness practitioner such a challenge is less about the suppression of unwanted thought, rather it seeks a more neutral "just noticing" that acknowledges that as thought arises, so eventually it will dissipate.

In recent studies focused on positive psychology much has been made of the role of flow or fluidity as an optimal state in which a person is able to access a greater sense of personal happiness and creativity. Somewhat paradoxically mindfulness practice appears to enable this through a greater acceptance of life's unpredictability and the sense of uncertainty that this can cause for us. With its historic roots in a Buddhist philosophy that saw the challenging nature of life as being unavoidable, mindfulness practice seeks to provide us with skills for managing our internal struggles more effectively.

Mindfulness practice is far from imagining utopias or having to adopt beliefs that jar with our experience of reality. In contrast it lays down the rather stark challenge of staying with the present moment, and what arises for us in that moment.

Interpersonal Benefits:
We already looked at the way in which mindfulness practice loosens up perceptions of ourselves and the thoughts that we have. Given that so many of our thoughts and judgements concern others, it is little surprise that developing self-awareness shifts how we experience other people.

Research in this field indicates that many practitioners report an increased sense of compassion and empathy towards other people. This may be due to people having increased capacity to listen to others, due to stress being reduced. Personally we have noticed that as we become more curious about ourselves, so that curiosity extends to other people rather than relying on prejudice or assumption.

One benefit that is especially pertinent to group mindfulness practice is the sense of community that the practice creates. During the course of a ten-week Mindfulness programme that Julian and I taught, a number of the participants identified themselves as people who used local mental health resources. This is a population that has often had to deal with being socially marginalised. A number of participants reported the helpfulness of having a setting where psychological skills could be learnt without there being any assumption about diagnosis or labels. We were all there simply because we wanted to practise.

This issue of community (or "Sangha" within the Buddhist tradition) is one that non-denominational mindfulness practice is beginning to address. We should not underestimate the counter-cultural force of a group of people willing to slow down! While not wanting to burden anyone with continuing a group or a programme ad infinitum, issues of sustainability need to be considered. In the process of our programme's evolution we provided the group with a resource sheet that highlighted other resources (from a wide variety of perspectives) that people might wish to explore.

Cultural Benefits:

If Mindfulness practice allows us to slow down and to become more aware of our preconceptions and judgements, it is highly likely that it will allow us to engage with art, history and culture with a new pair of eyes. Greater awareness far from leading to a preoccupation with altered states of consciousness, can lead us in adopting the "beginner's Mind" of the Zen tradition.

Our enthusiasm for bringing Mindfulness into public and cultural spaces was based firstly on a desire to emphasise its psychological value detached from religious tradition, and secondly we wanted to provide a means for museums and galleries to recapture their identity as places of spirit.

Arguably, many of the challenges to wellness faced by our culture have their roots in isolation, cultural poverty and a sense of historical dislocation. At the risk of sounding grandiose, museums, galleries and other cultural spaces have a vital role in addressing these needs. Whether via an art show or a display about war-time gardening, our role is not to tell people what to think, rather it is to act as a catalyst to curiosity and reflection.

Conclusion:

If our magical practice is to have any significant impact on the world in which we live, it seems critical that it seeks to address these personal and collective spheres. By working with this "Ninth Gate" we continue to explore the sense of poise and flexibility that meditative practice can provide. Within this quietness our magic is both questioned and refined in the hope that its newfound subtlety renders it more effective.

SD

A Meditation on Chaos

The relationship of mindfulness meditation and ritual practice is something that we've written about before in this blog. In terms of the chaos magick style, mindfulness can be imagined as being the 'Ninth Gate', the vacuity of Kia in the centre of the chaosphere. It is the still point in the circle of chaos, the moment before a decision is made to move outwards along one of the innumerable arrows of possibility (though, to save ink, typically only eight rays are shown) and into a particular paradigm (or behaviour).

Chaos magick often seeks to deliberately throw us off balance (by asking us to enter into novel belief structures, by stirring the cauldron of the unconscious, and occasionally by doing bat-shit crazy practices) and so having a psychic place that we can return to and be still in is very valuable.

Mindfulness itself is also a process, and there are various states that can be encountered while we do it. These jhānas are described through various models within the Buddhist tradition, typically as states that arise when the mind is free from hindrances such as craving, aversion, sloth, agitation and doubt. These jhāna states can be pretty weird in themselves (with things like delusions of enlightenment, freaky experiences of universal bliss, and other wild forms of ideation taking place). These are phenomena that don't get mentioned very much within the contemporary vogue for using mindfulness as a therapeutic tool. Such states can be unsettling, ecstatic or just plain weird and may not be what you ordered; especially if you're doing mindfulness just to help you de-stress and relax! Sometimes when we encounter these states it may simply be time to stop mindfulness (or to change the structure of this practice) for a while.

Very pretty, but just focus on your breathing and it will go away...

Although I've suggested that mindfulness is the 'still point' in the whirling chaos of our lives, the paradox is that it is, of course, still a technique. At a meta-level (and it's the use of meta-level or systemic thinking that makes chaos magick such a great tool) the process of; 'sit, observe the breath, thoughts arise, notice them, return to observation of breath' is itself a type of 'trance' (or 'script'). Sure it aims to allow us to 'sit with' whatever is going on, but there may be times when silent mediation really isn't what you need*. In these circumstances it can be better to mindfully do something; washing up, sweeping the floor, bathing (which are natural acts of banishing) or gathering food, cooking, and chopping firewood (acts of nurturing). It's also sometimes helpful to try different types of sitting; sitting for ten minutes with short gaps between sessions can be helpful, try sitting with eyes open or half-closed and so on. These methods also help counter the belief that more (ie longer) is necessarily better. Sure vipassana works for some folks but, like with brushing one's teeth, sometimes little, gentle, and often works better than lots, hard, and irregularly.

That paradox; that mindfulness is a magical technique that aims just to allow things to be as they are (rather than trying to stamp our Will on reality), is the flipside of the fact that ritual practice and daily life (where we often have an intention of 'doing something') can also function like mindfulness if approached in the right way. Being 'in flow' within any activity (be it going for a walk, playing music or doing some wild ceremonial ritual) can provide many of the same benefits as mindfulness (from improved immune system function to cognitive enhancements such as increased working memory). The difference is that these activities often have some form of core message or intention embedded within them, whereas mindfulness meditation seeks only to explore how things appear to awareness in that moment.

As we explore mindfulness/flow in more detail we might experience forms of radical cognitive discontinuity (sometimes called enlightenment) where it seems that we've made some kind of global shift in perception. As a chaos magician I like to hold onto these moments of illumination gently and think of them as waves upon the shore of Self. Each wave remakes the coastline and certainly there are times when radical shifts of awareness (think of these as amazing landslides) take place. However, for as long as we are aware and identified as individual entities (people), new waves (new experiences) will beat upon the shore, allowing new features to emerge in the landscape (the narrative of Self). Mindfulness may significantly re-model our sense of self, leading us to be less attached to things, more aware of flow, and to change the overall shape of our personal narratives. But even the enlightened person continues to change, to learn and to grow.

So each moment of illumination is not a final goal, but the dawn of a new becoming.

JV

*And of course, there are times when, rather than attempting to sit with how things appear, we should instead be fucking angry. As magicians we aim to change the world from lead to gold and as both Pete Carroll and John Lydon put it, 'anger is an energy'.

Lines taken from the turning wheel of the year:

The autumn morning; heavy rain drops
from indigo swollen clouds.

Full sailed, the moon rides behind billowing
grey-blue clouds

The crystallised earth is illuminated by the
brazen winter sun.

The racing clouds of winter, impaled by a
technicolour arc.

Lilac clouds lifted from the sodden January
soil.

Snow crowning the high moor fades into a
white winter sky.

The brave blue sky of spring is a canvas for
the rushing clouds.

Spinning doves, dancing up the dawning
spring

The bright air of spring tingles with bird
song.

Tiny zigzagging lives pepper the warm air.

The Dog Star glitters above the dark,
turbulent river.

The song-lines of birds are threaded
between fat drops of rain.

Strange folding clouds; a murmuration of
starlings above the ancient bridge.
Daffodils sun-dance beneath a clear, cold,
lapis sky.
The air is faecal scented as our grain is
stirred into the soil.
Droplet jewels hang beneath unfurling
leaves.
Apple blossom humming with bees in the
hot May sun.
Jubilant flowers, set in lush green, shine in
the bright air.
Big drops of rain fade fast under a hot sun.
Blessed sun warms pale skin, summer is
here!
Buttercups shine like tiny yellow suns,
writing dazzling constellations on the
green.
Swifts etch a mandala of wing and song in
the sky.
Insects ponder in the night above the day-
warmed stone.
On the calm sea, gold pours across the
horizon.
Soft summer stars are scattered through
the deep blue night.

From sublime rock pools, waves of light are
mirrored on the cliffs.
Coruscating waves are pushed ashore by a
wild warm wind.
A warm mist, concealing thunder, hangs
above the wide green world.
Hungry moths gather round fat flowering
blooms.
Swelling on the trees, the fruit of the
bright solar fire.
The midsummer monsoon blesses our
green northern isles.
Waves shiver the sun-reaching crop as the
sky breathes.
The spools of harvest begin to appear in
the fields.
Beneath the implacable sun the fields are
burnished gold.
Skittering calls in the grass, and bronze
slow-worms on the path.
A growing gibbous moon glows in the
warm stone scented air.
Retreating, the warm sea strands gelatinous
life-forms.
Welcome falls the night rain that
rejuvenates the land.

Yellow leaves upon strandline of the year,
as the tide of summer turns.
In bright daylight a north wind rattles the
first fall of leaves.
Autumn comes to the valley, wrapped in
morning mist.
Fast falling rain outside transforms the
house into a dark, dry sanctuary.
Great grey ships run before the north
wind, attended by arrows of south-bound
geese.
The Harvest moon swells above the river,
and floods the land.
Rust tatters the chestnut trees, heavy with
swollen spiked fruits.
Muted colours on the land as the evening
light fades.
A cold, clear moon waxes in the west.
Wood smoke lingers in the chill air of
dawn.
This icy night the hunched moon unfolds a
great halo.
Day slides in between the wild sea and sky.
A wild-hunt of cloud announces the cold,
wet morning.
A wild-wind scatters the tattered leaves.

Sodden is the earth beneath the fallen
leaves.

The Spheres of Chaos

In addition to the eight Sabbats of Chaos Craft, another motif we've continued to use in our work has been that of the Five Spheres. This conceptual device developed by Pete Carroll in consultation with Nikki Wyrd, links to the vowel sounds (I, E, A, O, U) that are incorporated in the 'middle pillar' part of the Gnostic Banishing rituals. In these practices attention is given to the crown of the head (the Chaosphere), the throat (the Noosphere), the heart (the Anthrosphere), the belly (the Biosphere) and the perineum (the Geosphere).

The whole system is described in detail towards the end of *The Book of Baphomet.* Each sphere indicates a perspective from which we can view the world. There is no implicit hierarchy of 'sacredness' implied in the model. The conception of the spheres presented here is developed within the various esoteric discourses that are styled as being of 'The Left-hand Path'.

Geosphere

We've started a series of rituals to explore each sphere. The first in the sequence is the Geosphere; the world of the rocks, the stones and the crystals (as the old Pagan chant puts it). This is the place of the Elder Gods, and in the biological register, our sense of hunger.

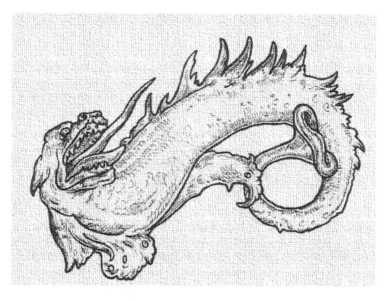

His snorting throws out flashes of light;
his eyes are like the rays of dawn.

Each ceremony itself (so far we've done three rites) has included simple shamanic style techniques; the use of poetic text, drumming and silent meditation. Our aim; to commune with these different interpretations or layers of reality, while bringing a distinctly Left Hand Path and Setian mindset to this work.

The Geosphere, imagined in terms of the life of a person, is our intrauterine and infantile existence. Looked at in cosmological terms, it is that great dyad of space and time. It another sense it is the realm of raw physics:

Hydrogen begat Helium,

Helium begat Carbon,

Carbon begat Oxygen

In terrestrial terms the symbol of this sphere is the equal armed cross + representing the physical earth upon which we stand. From the magnetosphere that shields us from the solar wind, down through the depths of the ocean, riding upon the backs of tectonic plates, and deeper, to the core of our planet (which glows at the same temperature as the surface of the sun). For our lived experience, as dwellers on the surface, it is the four directions, the crossroads.

The spirit of this sphere (in a Typhonian stylee) is the monster Leviathan and the poem we used is taken from The Book of Job. It is also the place of Apep or Apophis, the great dragon-serpent whom Set keeps at bay, protecting the sun in its nightly journey through the underworld. I sometimes imagine Apophis as entropy, that mighty stooping dragon who, within the narrative of the cosmological Standard Model, seeks to drag down complexity into a vast uniform heat death of elementary particles and radiations. Space and time gives birth to all things, and in the end (it seems) will also be the tomb of everything. The all-potential womb is also the all-embracing tomb.

But for all this, biology and mind rises up (like Set) against (and within) this inky black darkness. We are mud that sat up and became sensate.

(In a perhaps less Setian style, one might also point out that the universe, for all its faults, seems peculiarly adapted to the needs of the kind of physics and chemistry that allows for life.

Our cosmos seems perfectly set up not only to permit but to encourage life. Were the weak force (or the others in that great fundamental quadruplicity) just a little weaker, and it could all have gone horribly wrong.)

JV

(Recordings related to the work of The Spheres of Chaos can be located in Julian Vayne's bit of Soundcloud.com).

Biosphere

The second realm in our sequence of The Spheres of Chaos is the Biosphere; the seething, fornicating, birthing and dying world of life. As the raw material of the Geosphere held the emergent complexity of life embedded as an implicate (and perhaps inevitable) force within it, so the Biosphere is the space within which our bodies are formed. It is in the next sphere, the Anthrosphere, that the centrality of humans and the products of our behaviours are described. But, as it says in *The Book of Baphomet*, 'The Anthrosphere emerges from the Biosphere and remains critically dependent on it'. When we consider all life (using the model of the Five Spheres) we simultaneously acknowledge that we are part of this life, we are biological beings and also (and here comes that Setian LHP vibe folks), that in some respects humans are radically different from the rest of Nature.

The twin serpent of DNA spins and twists, coding out millions of forms in continuously changing, morphing, mutating profusion. The constants of the physical world anchor this wild multiplicity through adaptation to the environment. The sea of the late Triassic looked much like the sea of today and so the phenotype of ichthyosaurus reminds us of modern dolphins. Flesh adapts to the world in which it finds itself. One wave of gigantic reptilian life dies off (perhaps destroyed by a meteoric hammer blow) and new creatures flood in to the fill the evolutionary gaps. Ice Ages cover the Geosphere; life responds by getting all big and hairy. But this relationship goes both ways. Through the subduction and cycling of the earth's mantle, the products of biology are folded within our planet. Coal and oil, the sleeping shadows of ancient life, rest deep in the earth. Flint, made from the bodies of ancient creatures, chalk sifted from the bones of innumerable archaic snails. And not only echoes of life, there's plenty of living things a long, long way down. Even high up in the atmosphere (itself a mix of gases produced by biological activity) tiny critters populate the skies. Our whole planet is touched by life.

The symbol connected with this sphere is the two-point up pentagram, sigil of Baphomet and of The Devil. Given the biological focus of this sphere we decided to work with this spirit as Pan, all devourer and all-begetter. A God who appears in the sylvanian landscape of childhood's dream as *The Piper at the Gates of Dawn*, and as the archaic form of wild sexual frenzy in Arthur Machen's *The Great God Pan*.

With hoofs of steel I race on the rocks

The invocation we used in this work was of Aleister Crowley's wonderful Hymn to Pan, one of the finest ritual poems of the 20th century. This was used as part of our ceremony.

Drumming, scourging, drinking and general wildness are perfect methods for connecting to this sphere. The Biosphere witnesses our lust for life!

JV

Anthrosphere

The heart of the Spheres of Chaos model is the Anthrosphere, also known as the Opusphere (the world of the works of humanity) or the Technosphere. Here we recognise the peculiar way in which we, *Homo sapiens*, influence the Geosphere and Biosphere. With our amazing ability to make and control fire we have literally changed every part of the planet. One example of this is the way in which archaeologists, when using radio carbon dating techniques, give dates as 'BP' meaning Before Present. And when is the present exactly? The answer is January 1st 1950; following our detonation of the first atomic bombs we've spread radioactive isotopes across the whole world. After 1950 the carbon dating system is screwed, no dates established using that technique after that year can be trusted (and this will apply for a very, very long time).

This is the reason why, in geological terms, the era we're living in is called the Anthropocene - a period that many scientists consider begins with the industrial revolution. In the Anthrosphere we appreciate ourselves as deeply technological entities, throwing off tools, structures, wastes and behaviours into the world. Our technology circles the planet, looking back with unblinking satellite eye on the Geopshere and Biosphere. Techniques including animal domestication, farming, vaccination and written language have allowed us to proliferate in great numbers.

Our biology itself is profoundly influenced by our technology; humans are coctivores, our gut's structure reflects our millennia long love of cooked food. We change our bodies with piercing, tattooing, pharmaceuticals, artificial limbs and Google glasses.

The god of this centre (in our Left Hand Path analysis of the Spheres) is Set. Here is the god who is an exemplar of our deviation and division from other life-forms in the Biosphere. Set's symbols include the knife and the scissors, those implements we use to cut the cord between the mother and child. Set is typically imagined as a bit kinky, a bit weird (in Norse culture we might say he is a bit *ergi*). He is god of the exotic, of metals, and of oil. He is associated with the colour red. The colour of hot, glowing iron from which we forge our tools and our machines.

Brave new world

Our work with Set and the Anthrosphere consisted of a freestyle shamanic opening up, to allow communication with this power. To do this we pulled out all the techno-esoteric stops; strobe lights, smoke machine, and *Die Elektischen Vorspiele* (an excellent track used in the rituals of The Temple of Set).

How do we acknowledge the 'Gift of Set', our individuating Self, while at the same time appreciating that we are nourished by, and depend on others (other people, the

Biosphere and Geosphere)? This is the great challenge of our species.

JV

Noosphere

Lucifer, that bright Son of the Morning, teaches in Crowley's poem that 'the key to joy is disobedience'. What does this mean? In the context of The Spheres of Chaos we worked with the Luciferian spirit (this time using bodywork and trance dance, rooting us in the other three spheres) to explore the Noosphere. The Noosphere is the realm of ideas, of complex language. It is the world where, quite literally, nothing is true and everything is permitted. We can create paradoxes and word plays that disobey the material strictures of the previous realms of the Geosphere, Biosphere and Anthrosphere. All communications are lies, edits of reality, cut-ups, impossible visions.

I can tell you that there is an object that is a black flame. A statement that makes sense in language and yet, when we really set to imagine what that means, is pretty tricky. What about if I tell you that there is an object that is totally red and also totally yellow? Again the words make sense but the object cannot be easily imagined. And, away from the realm of objects, things become even more unruly. In the beginning was the word that, especially in its written form, was a *pharmakon*.

Strike a Light!

Language, with its set of fairly simple rules, gives rise to unending complexity. Analogous to the way DNA operates we speak of memes, concepts that flow through the Noosphere. The Noosphere is the network, the web of communications that now span the entire globe. It is the messages, the truth and lies, the ever-shifting perspective of cultures. The realm of ideas is limitless and, though our thoughts are undoubtedly grounded in our physicality as humans, our language, our ideas spawn new forms and allow us to understand ourselves in new ways. Algorithmic intelligence, sifting our big data, has been achieved. Artificial intelligence may not be far behind. I wonder what will happen when our machines come alive, or when we have interfaced with them even more pervasively and deeply? When we are fully embedded in the flow of a global conversation?

In terms of our human 'break' from the Biosphere, it is not language itself that marks us apart, but the complexity of the way in which we do it. More than this, writing (a skill that lay sleeping in human neurology for perhaps hundreds of thousands of years) popped up, in a crazy aeonic style, in a number of places on our planet within a few centuries of each other. Writing is the gift of Lucifer. Promethean, we have stolen the fire from heaven. The god-like ability to make worlds with our words.

Just like Lucifer (our fallen angel) the energy (for want of better word) of this sphere is a descending one. It has a stellar quality, perhaps connecting it to our astronomical sciences that inform that (apparently) universal language of mathematics. Numbers and calculation (the basis of Statecraft; to run a large culture counting and detailed record keeping is essential) are the probable origin of writing. Though we might like to claim that Thoth invented writing, it seems the first evidence for human literary production is not religious texts or poetry but rather shopping lists and tax returns.

Ideas floating around in the Noosphere include things like 'the self'. This psychic structure is the narrative attached to our bodies but which emerges in large part from our interaction with others; we are this conversation conducted within and around us.

JV

Chaosphere

This page is intentionally void of content.

Initiation
Stirring the Cauldron

Julian and I were recently chatting about our own initiatory experiences that related to undertaking intensive periods of magical practice and training. In this case it was *Liber MMM* from *Liber Null and Psychonaut*.

Me: "How's Bob getting on with MMM?"
Julian: "Yeah pretty well, lots of great diary work but things do seem to be unravelling a bit for him personally..."
Me: "Do you know anyone that this process hasn't shaken up in a major way?"
Julian: (thoughtful pause) "... ah... No, I guess that's what it's supposed to do!"

It seems my Christian friends were right, Magick is dangerous. These technologies are designed to plunge elbow deep into your unconscious and give it an almighty stir. As much as results magick might produce quantifiable change "out there", it seems undeniable that the major locus of magickal activity and change is 'in here', "in consciousness according to Will" (Dion Fortune). If it's stability you're seeking stay away from religious and spiritual traditions that have a major magickal component (and that's most of them) - you're only going to upset your Self.

Fire burn, and cauldron bubble...

This stirring of ourselves potentially disturbs not only material that we may have suppressed into our personal unconscious, but it may touch upon shared ancestral memories. None of us come into the world as blank pages; we come with the genetic load of our ancestors and we are born into cultural settings that define us from the very point of conception. As we engage in the type of transformational work that most magical curricula lay out, it seems likely that we will need to address issues 'within' ourselves, but also relationships and the contextual conditioning that have shaped the self-image with which we are currently engaging.

Personally I think being upset can be a good thing, temporary abandonments of apparent sanity (whatever that might be) allowing us to avoid complete meltdown. Magick often provides the psychological equivalent of dynamiting the San Andreas Fault to prevent a major earthquake. Such a metaphor does however raise the question of how much explosives to use!

During my own involvement with magick there have been definite periods where I have experienced a type of Gnostic burnout or overload where I have had to take my foot off the gas and seek far gentler pursuits. In many forms of psychotherapy (my day job) one of the primary dialectics which needs to be held in tension, is that which exists between acceptance and change. If all therapy does is accept, it will never be truly healing, and if all it does is ask for change without truly listening to reality as it is for the client, then it is both an imposition and a misuse of power. How, in my spiritual life, can I access this place of acceptance rather than bleeding myself psychically dry through endless sorcerous 'doing'?

All this has got me thinking about the wisdom of spiritual paths that seek to view magic as part of a more holistic sadhana or spiritual practice. My own development has been greatly inspired by the fourth Way work of Gurdjieff and Ouspensky, that seek to harmonise the path of gnosis (the way of the Yogi) with that of the embodied wisdom (the way of the Fakir) and also the bhakti path of devotion (the way of the Monk). At the risk of sounding like a bad chaos magician I wonder whether the pursuit of magick outside of a spiritual or religious context is sustainable or even desirable. Perhaps what I'm grappling with is the importance of having a symbol set that has been deeply internalised, so that when our self-induced shape shifting intensifies, we have a psychic map via which we can get a better sense of our bearings.

Even when armed with such portentous warnings, we can still end up flattened by the spiritual shock waves that focused spiritual activity can induce. During my own work with *Liber MMM* over 5 years ago, I undertook an intensive piece of devotional work connected to the dark mother figure Sekhmet from the Egyptian pantheon. My motivations for undertaking this work were complex, but needless to say that after a prolonged focus on this wrathful, lion-headed goddess I ended up feeling both devoured and dismembered. I felt emotionally hollowed out and was psychologically confused to the extent that I took a several month leave of absence from the magical group with which I was working.

Surviving such spiritual crises can be a tricky endeavour, but I think that the following factors were helpful in helping me find a way through:

Magical colleagues who were wise enough not to pressure me and were able to normalise my experience. Whether framed as a "dark night of the soul" or an abyss type experience, periods of disorientation and psychic exhaustion are exceedingly common for those pursuing paths that use radical means. Having a network of supportive chums telling you that you will get through it helps.

Returning to core practice that sustains you. When I felt broken, I returned to stillness and bodywork. Mindfulness meditation and gentle yoga practice allowed me to ground myself again rather than seeking to extend further via more active sorcery or divination.

Letting go of the project. The "lust for results" can be as much about the project of self-improvement or awakening as it can be about sorcery. Sometimes we need to lean towards accepting things as they are rather than continually pushing for change. Paradoxically, it often feels that when we slip into that "neither-neither", non-dual state of awareness and rest, that a new sense of freedom and openness can be experienced.

SD

Thoughts on Initiation

I was chatting to a friend recently about her deepening involvement with Vajrayāna Buddhism and whether she should take the initiatory step of formally taking refuge. Her dilemma was whether to "enter the stream" of the tradition or simply continue to benefit from the techniques being taught. For me this highlighted some questions that I've been musing on with regards the nature of what initiation is, and how it may (or may not) be of benefit.

Arguably, the moment we direct our will and intention towards spiritual or psychological change, we are undertaking initiatory work. From such a perspective each moment in daily life can become an opportunity for transformation. However valid such an approach, as someone who chooses to utilise the tools of ritual and other magical technologies, I believe that such change can be more actively pursued and intensified. But why go to all this bother? What is it that I'm really hoping to gain through this investment of time, energy and money? Why not just spend more time surfing? What follows are the beginnings of some answers:

1. Knowledge.

Wizards have always loved books. Checking out the work of Owen Davies we can see that by owning books and even possibly knowing what's inside them, the magician acquires prestige and thus power. Times really haven't changed have they? A quick scan of my friends on Facebook tells me that most of us love weird tomes, the more expensive and obscure the better! Rather than wanting to debate the merits of the current trend in talismanic publishing, I'm more interested in what it might represent in relation to people's search for (cue spooky sound effects) "initiated knowledge".

As we seek to explore the deeper aspects of both ourselves and the universe, it's understandable that we should seek expertise in navigating these occult realms. Whatever the credentials and affiliations of such authors, are there real limits to what can be conveyed magically through the written word alone? As many of us spend more time typing, texting and liking, it's easy to dismiss the idea that certain wisdom can only be conveyed via direct relationship. The Kabbalistic maxim "from mouth to ear" for me conveys something of the person specific tailoring that most deep engagement with a tradition seems to entail. In the context of psychotherapy, Carmel Flaskas speaks of the importance of being "Witnessed"- a sense of being truly seen by the other. There is something profoundly transformational about real interpersonal connection - perhaps even more as we seek to develop soul. This may be about the sharing of some great wisdom, but it might be as much about real presence whilst having a beer together.

2. Collective Identity.

Even for those of us fortunate enough to be part of a regular coven, lodge or working group, it may well be that the majority of our practice is carried out in a solitary context. This may feel fitting given the degree of consciousness needed in order to strike out on a magical path, but for many of us such isolationism rarely sustains the project. However a specific tradition expresses its collectivism, for me one of the key components to initiation is that it is into a community.

Within the Buddhist tradition sangha, or the community of practitioners, is one of the three treasures (along with the Buddha and dharma). This is a key recognition that for a spiritual path to be sustainable it needs to have a sense of the collective. The parameters around a community will vary from tradition to tradition - some may emphasise ascent to a core set of ideas e.g. Thelema, others may emphasise adherence to a type of counter-cultural tribalism (some Chaos Magickal groups adopt this pattern). Whatever the social glue that emerges during the life of a tradition, what seems to be important for people giving their allegiance to such systems is the sense of trans-personal purpose in feeling the weight of the group's history, its current egregore/group mind and the potential teleos often connected to its role in some sort of aeonic unfolding!

As someone who has worked within several initiatory traditions I recognise both the strength and potential danger connected with stepping inside the 'inner court' of their processes. The Kaula Nath tradition that I've worked within for the last ten years is a path that emphasises the connection between tribal identity and initiation (one of the primary meanings of Kaula being clan). Such initiatory families can be a source of support, security and necessary balance, but they can also reflect the less helpful aspects of family life. All families run to scripts - we rely on often unspoken principles and roles in order to create a sense of certainty and continuity. In and of themselves such scripts are not necessarily negative, but what happens if we want to try something new, or re-negotiate our role within the tribe? Along with John Byng-Hall I'd agree that the litmus test for the health of any group seems to be whether we are permitted the reflective space to name the scripts and improvise new ways of being.

3. Direct Transmission.

The late Georg Feuerstein highlighted that in the tantric tradition, initiation could take many forms varying from prolonged preparation and elaborate ritual, to the lightning flash of the guru staring into the core of ones being. While the advent of skype etc. might make cyber-initiations a useful tool if travel is not possible, for me there is something both potent and fundamentally congruent about initiation taking place in the flesh. For a child to be healthy in early life it needs to be held and truly seen by its care giver - should the needs of the spiritual new-born be any less? Whether our initiation is into the group-mind of an Order or the familial lineage of a guru, it seems that the most powerful transmissions occur via the direct activation of the body, mind and emotions.

For those of us who've spent more than their fair share of time lost in the spiritual supermarket, the location of a teacher or a well-balanced tradition can feel like the goal itself rather than the beginning that it actually represents. Any group or guru worth their salt should come with a health warning - if they don't make at least some effort to put you off I'd be worried. A good friend likened initiation to being like spiritual dynamite! This seems to be in keeping with Feuerstein's observation; "the guru's work with disciples is both a demolition job and a rebuilding." Indeed! As someone who has sought and undergone a number of initiatory processes, they definitely accelerate a process of change. Be careful what you wish for!

SD

Sources:

John Byng-Hall *Re-writing Family Scripts* (Guilford Press 1995)

Owen Davies *Ordinary Magic* (Hambeldon Continuum 2007)

Georg Feuerstein *Tantra* (Shambhala 1998)

Carmel Flaskas *Family Therapy Beyond Postmodernism* (Brunner-Routledge 2002)

Geoffrey Samuel *The Origins of Yoga and Tantra* (Cambridge 2008)

Check out enfolding.org

Chaos Craft Initiation Ritual

Preparation: The Candidate has worked with the Craft of Chaos method for at least one year and decided that they would like to formally mark their work in context of the group. Moreover they have determined that they wish to instigate an initiatory process within themselves. This ritual thus has a group-context meaning and an inner, personal, spiritual process.

In immediate preparation for this ritual the Candidate follows a self-created program of work to explore each of the Five Spheres of Chaos. Four such experiments are recorded in this volume, while more detail of the whole system can be found in *The Book of Baphomet*).

On the altar is a vessel of anointing oil. A chalice is present containing red wine.

The circle is cast deosil (starting at the direction appropriate to the time of the year at which the working is being done). Each of the eight directions are honoured and their powers brought into the circle.)

The candidate leaves the room and is asked to meditate for a while.

The candidate is led in, naked, bound and hoodwinked.

They are challenged with a knife against their breast by the Gatekeeper; 'Candidate, what do you seek?'

Candidate: 'I seek the Mysteries'. (Or other suitable words as you Will.)

Gate Keeper: 'Then are you ready to undergo the Ordeal?'

Candidate: 'Yes'

The candidate is then helped to kneel. They are scourged 7, 2, and 9 times.

(A singing bowl is rung before each battery of scourges and once at the end of the process.)

The candidate is unbound and the hoodwink is removed.

The Priest then says: 'Candidate, speak to us of the Geosphere'

The candidate does so; at the end of their words the group (including the candidate) sing the sound 'U'. After each sound the Priest anoints the candidate with the eight-fold star at the appropriate point on the body.

This is repeated for all five of the spheres.

The candidate then kneels and the Priest uses the Barbaric invocation of Baphomet (from *The Gates of Baphomet* rite). Each point is then touched as the invocation is given.

There is then a space for the candidate to reveal the Mystery [drumming and dance].

Wine is offered. The candidate holds the cup. All chant 'Baphomet, Witchblood, her blood, his blood'.

The candidate drinks. The chalice is then passed from the candidate to the Priest with the offer 'My blood, your blood'.

The chalice is passed around until all have drunk.

The Candidate takes another drink as the chalice returns to them and declares: 'I am <name> a <title> of the Craft of Chaos!'

Cheers of delight from the assembled multitude.

Chaos Craft

Acknowledging our Selves as Baphomet

At the end of many of the Chaos Craft rituals the members of the coven sit together, cross-legged in a circle. We begin by holding hands (because that's always nice) and take three breaths together. (For the sky above us, for the earth beneath us, and for the water surrounding our island of Britain. This technique is borrowed from modern Druidry.) Participants then raise their right hand towards the sky, their left hand pointing towards the ground.

We say together:

"From the Heights of the Heavens..." (looking up, right)

"To the Depths of the Earth..." (looking down, left)

Folding hands together over our own chest, say:

"We are one Heart."

Reaching out to either side to touch the hearts of those sitting beside us, say:

"Connected."

So Mote It Be!

Also by the same author(s):

Seeds of Magick: An Expose of Modern Occult Practices, Catherine Summers and Julian Vayne. 1991, Llewellyn Publications.

The Inner Space Workbook, Catherine Summers and Julian Vayne. 1994, Capall Bann Publishing.

Personal Development with the Tarot, Catherine Summers and Julian Vayne. 2002, Foulsham (2nd edition).

Now That's What I Call Chaos Magick, Julian Vayne and Greg Humphries. 2004, Mandrake.

Pharmakon: Drugs and the Imagination, Julian Vayne. 2006, Mandrake of Oxford.

Magick Works: Stories of Occultism in Theory and Practice, Julian Vayne. 2008, Mandrake of Oxford.

The Book of Baphomet, Julian Vayne and Nikki Wyrd. 2012, Mandrake of Oxford.

Wonderful Things - Learning with Museum Objects, Julian Vayne. 2012, MuseumsEtc.

Deep Magic: Tales and Techniques of Practical Occultism, Julian Vayne. 2013, Mandrake of Oxford.

Chaos Craft: The Wheel of the Year in Eight Colours, Julian Vayne and Steve Dee. 2015, The Universe Machine.

...and of course, The Blog of Baphomet - theblogofbaphomet.com

Made in the USA
Columbia, SC
09 March 2018